# THE HUMAN REINVENTION FORMULA

Escape Burnout
Create Sustainable Wealth
Join the New Breed of Superheroes

By
**Mia Munro**

First published in 2019 by Mia Munro
Sunshine Coast, QLD

© Mia Munro
The moral rights of the author have been asserted.
This book is a SpiritCast Network book.

---

**Author:** Munro, Mia

**Title:** The Human Reinvention Formula; Escape Burnout, Create Sustainable Wealth, Join the New Breed of Superheroes

**ISBN:** 978-1-698-19465-3

**Editor-in-chief:** Anita Saunders

**Cover Designs:** Sarah Rose Design

---

**Disclaimer:**

The material in this publication is of the nature of general comment only, and does not represent professional advice. It is not intended to provide specific guidance for particular circumstances and it should not be relied on as the basis for any decision to take action or not take action on any matter which it covers. Readers should obtain professional advice where appropriate, before making any such decision. To the maximum extent permitted by law, the author and publisher disclaim all responsibility and liability to any person, arising directly or indirectly from any person taking or not taking action based on the information in this publication.

**My wish for you**

May you always know your uniqueness
Your strength and tenacity
Your determination
Never give up

When you are tested
Know the gift of growth
Grow with a vulnerable heart
Never shame your soul
For it knows your truth

Feel the darkness
Own your light

Trust beyond this human existence
To a world beyond your mind's view
Feel that passion
Own your vision
For you are powerful beyond belief

May you reinvent yourself
Over and over again

Unpack with honesty
Disrupt truthfully
Upgrade authentically

With each cell in your body
Your heart bursts with light
Your soul singing its own song
Reinvent you!

**Mia Munro**

# FOREWORD

## Create Deliberate Choices—Create Enriched Lives

It is an honour to be supported by so many incredible human beings who are transitioning through life creating profound ripple effects. Some of these are powerful leaders known to many and some are silent leaders doing incredible work without the title or status. I honour them equally and thank them for their inspiration, their life's work, and most of all, their sacred souls! We are all a part of one whole. I see a future when we do not need more gurus operating from ego in the limelight. We need to become our own guru. We need communities enriched with many embodied humans. And new global agendas. This is my mission!

A few words from my peers ...

*Mia is a dear friend and I believe epitomises a powerful feminine version of a warrior. I have been blessed to be beside her through many chapters and challenges that she has endured and risen above. She refuses to give up. Her determination to embrace each life crisis and learn from it is magnificent to observe. Her new project,* The Human Reinvention Formula, *is set to turn old paradigms on their head. It's her time, speaking out about what she experiences. Few have the courage to stand for real change. We have a common interest in the protection of those at risk and we align in standing together for world-changing projects. You can expect to read a powerful book that transcends societal constructs and allows humans to find a freedom that most crave. I commend Mia on her ventures and look forward to joining her when she hits the USA.*

**Simon Treselyan**
**Author and Inspirational Speaker**

*I met Mia Munro in 2004 during her engagement in one of my Australian events. She was a very determined woman, ready to break through her limitations. She has never stopped taking action towards her dreams. She has gone on to become an author, build a seven-figure business in the wealth creation industry, and now tours as a speaker internationally with her philosophies alongside her philanthropic projects. Through the many stages required to upgrade one's self she has continued to rise as an unstoppable leader. Her new book,* The Human Reinvention Formula, *is set to be a bestseller and I highly commend her commitment to humanity.*

**Chris Howard**
**CEO Million Dollar Mastermind**

*Working in partnership with Mia Munro within my Amazon education business has proved to be fruitful. Her dynamic attitude to business and human transformation has meant she has been able to reinvent herself to new heights in a very short time frame. Her new book is exactly what humans need right now with so many leaders falling into exhaustion. Her formula makes sure that we walk a deliberate pathway to create a life that is sustainable in energy and aligned to our truth. Her background in human transformation complements many wealth creation models through identifying limiting behaviours that impact results. Her formula is a practical and deliberate approach to transcending past failures and a breakthrough opportunity to build wealth and a more enriched life.*

**Sophie Howard**
**Bluesky Amazon Sellers Academy**

*The world is full of specialists, technical experts and people who love to complicate things. One day I had the opportunity to meet and work with Mia and I saw something rather unique and different in her character. We were both presenting different unique strategies on stage about building wealth around Australia without the need to complicate things or create chaos.*

*From meeting Mia, it was clear that she is a very passionate woman on a mission to see people grow and expand, just like I have been over the last 15 years and we clicked. Mia has a very open mind and great experience in identifying the alignment of wealth strategies with an individuals strengths. What stood out was her desire to collaborate and work together for the greater good of all involved.*

*I was aware of her challenging background however I could see the determination and passion to push through that, and it did not stop her soaring in a short space of time, all thanks I believe to her Human Reinvention Formula.*

*I am honoured to work together with Mia and see a very bright future ahead for those who choose to follow her formula to create great wealth coupled with a reinvented self.*

**George Fokas**
**Investor | Global Wealth Mentor | Educator**
**| Key Note Speaker**

*We met Mia in early 2019 whilst on a speaking tour where we shared stages around Australia. We had the opportunity to witness her present her passion of creating multiple streams of income with models that disrupt the mainstream way of doing business. Post tour she was hit with being unwell and yet she powered through her next stage of reinvention to write this book. Without a doubt, Mia has a strength inside her to continue to elevate herself beyond the norm. We currently partner with Mia in two businesses both which are a new way of doing business and are behind her next level approach to reinvention. Her new book is set to become a best seller and we hope to connect with her community to share disruptive opportunities in the future,*

**Aaron and Nicole Byrelee**
**BnB Professionals**

*In 2011/12 Mia showed up in my life, in Bali, a bit beaten up from a failed business partnership that saw her lose her company. At the same time she was finding inspiration for the next chapter of her life, showing up real, raw and naked, being totally vulnerable and sharing her journey openly. I remember thinking how courageous this young woman was, how resilient and committed she was to showing others that when we are in our vulnerability we are in our power, in our commitment to pick ourselves up is the power to move others, in our sharing is our healing, and the inspired healing for others. What you can always trust you'll get from Mia is the truth, unaltered, uncensored, real and raw, delivered from a beautiful feminine, heartfelt and honouring place that uplifts, inspires and empowers you to take positive action.*

**John Abbott**
**Audience Awakening**
**Inspiral**

# MESSAGE FROM MIA

In a world full of human beings living big and diverse lives, we see the rise and fall of many. But few get back up and decisively continue to lead an incredible life full of extraordinary experiences. Many of my mentors and peers have played a big game of life. And most of them have crashed, fallen, or been taken down by others. It seems inevitable.

Whilst living in Australia, I have experienced the well-known tall poppy syndrome; I have been bullied, attacked, and judged. I have been shamed and lost all faith in humanity many times. I have become a victim and have risen through adversity.

But I have never given up.

I refuse to live in fear of this thing called life. I own my power. I engage in relationships that uplift me and support my highest good. I respect those that honour my boundaries and am clear for those still learning this. I value those who are bold enough to be truthful and am open to collaboration of the purest kind. I operate out of integrity—it is my highest value. I hope for more of this in the human race.

I am as human as they come; with training wheels on, I am learning every day. I get tripped up and then I soar in magnificence. I have been taken into the trenches, rock bottom and what felt like ground zero, but I have not died. I stand taller and stronger than ever before; with each moment of challenge I am constantly expanding! This is my mission for you.

Do not be fooled into thinking I have it all sorted; I do not choose that pedestal. I would rather stand beside you. I find being human hard some days. I feel pain, I hurt, and I cry often. I am a deeply sensitive woman and I do care greatly for humans, animals, and our environment.

I am weird, I don't fit in, and I probably never will. But I am mastering this human experience and I come with great wisdom. I have fallen and I have risen! I am deeply creative, feminine, and take my work to the world from this place. The masculine has been honoured and the integration is ongoing. But this call is from my feminine spirit who needs to be nurtured so much more this time around.

This is my reinvention 7.0 and I have no doubt there are many more to come.

This book is a statement, a philosophy, and a guide for those of you who may have fallen or are about to. You may be exhausted by life. An exhaustion beyond activity, a deep wasting away of your life force, and you know that there is a radical need for change. Many parts of your whole self may be out of whack. But where do you start when it's so hard to see a way forward?

This formula will guide you through a clear, succinct, and powerful structure, reviewing all parts of you, through your wealth creation vehicles, your relationship with self, the energetic system of your body, your community involvement or contribution work. We will delve into them all. I will share openly my stories to allow you to see concepts in the form of metaphors. My ego does not need these stories to be shared; rather, they serve a purpose.

Will you take the plunge into truth and rise too?

This is one of the greatest opportunities we have as humans, a chance to reset, uplevel, or even reinvent ourselves.

And this book is written to guide you towards a profound shift in your reality. Your own unique shift. If I was to assume I know exactly what you need then I would be operating from an egoic standpoint. That is not what we need here. This process will begin to take you home to you.

I have witnessed many people go through trauma, heartbreak, abuse, major disasters, and loss and failure in business. The majority remain in the last stage they fell within.

They remain traumatised, living with PTSD daily, they never love again, they remain disempowered, they never trust or feel safe, and never take their businesses to the next level.

And I am as human as they come. But there is one thing that has been brought to my attention. I never stay down for long and I transcend beyond each reality after every challenge. I literally reinvent myself. And I am sure you recognise this in yourself too.

I have done life quite solo at times and so my best advisor has been me. In fact, when I have looked to others for answers and listened and followed without discernment I have ended up creating more trauma. I relied on others' wisdom at times instead of listening to my own. We always know what is best for us if we listen carefully.

So over the last 45 years I have crashed many times, lost many people I love, had my heart broken, felt like giving up, experienced fraud in business, natural disasters, and the list goes on ... And for every crash I have risen up. And this book is the formula I have used over and over and it has been upgraded many times as I have upgraded within myself. This is a continual process which becomes a smooth and more aligned way to expand life.

*So, how do we make the most of this human life when we are so very often challenged by external forces, conformity, societal systems, and ways of living that do not actually align to us?*

# REINVENTION
*requires a multifaceted approach*

This book is for wise and self-responsible humans who are prepared to question what is important right now for the benefit of their own happiness and life. They are open to delve into truth and are ready to disrupt old paradigms.

This is not a book for those who refuse to change, trolls who spend their days bullying others, or those who choose to use this information to create anti-campaigns. There is enough darkness in this world. You need to own your patterns, your disappointments, and your wounding in every stage. One will never grow without this.

This formula must not be misunderstood as some radical projection on my part. It has been brought through with care and it has multiple layers which we can delve into through our other opportunities to connect.

You won't see fluffy unicorns or woohoo escapism, you will experience real deepening within yourself; you may experience discomfort, life may feel confused and disorientated, and you might be seriously challenged to slow down to speed up.

And …

Through this process you may find deep peace, new ways of creating abundance, and most of all JOY!

Your heart will open wide to new possibilities, your mind will work with your needs to allow for expansion, you will experience magical moments that remind you of what life is really all about, life will gain clarity and moments of complete joy.

My intention in every story I share and the knowledge I have gained is to present it from my perspective, a woman who has loved boldly, experienced major trauma, and is wide awake in a crazy world. I come from a place of acceptance for what is; I am not apathetic but I also do not believe fighting against darkness for light has ever really helped. I have been tested over and over in life. Do I take on the fight or rise up higher? In every case I have chosen to rise higher. Acting out of principles in life has become irrelevant. I care about my human experience more than the energy wasted on blame games! In the stories I share, I do not blame anyone. I would never defame any other human despite how much pain some behaviours have created. I know the pain that causes, I have experienced that from others.

I will not engage in polarisation or aligning to corrupt systems that try and control our human race. I believe in personal disruption as a powerful concept as a beginning stage. I see too many external disruptors forget about the importance of self, becoming martyrs to their work.

To discover my own beliefs and to stand tall in my own philosophies has given me much strength. I wish that you may live freely without the fear-mongering strategies affecting your ability to sleep at night. I wish you to live a life with reduced stress and more enjoyment. You can live a version of life that fulfils your real needs when you look outside the conformity and false realities being shown to you.

I have lived free of traditional work for over 15 years now; I have lived in my favourite locations on islands or holiday destinations, choosing to be based in paradise rather than slog it out in busy and polluted cities. I have chosen to eat the food I really need for many years and treat my body naturally in the first instance, only tapping into the medical system for emergencies.

I have chosen to live in other countries in the East and live a different type of life and culture. I see beauty in the East and the West. They both bear gifts that we can acknowledge and integrate.

I have been able to choose my relationships to be of a certain kind and model. My communities will be ever evolving. Some would say I have lived a transient lifestyle but I have chosen to shift communities when they did not serve an alignment to my belief systems and change relationships as they cease to evolve with love. I feel and listen in to what I need next. The judgement on these decisions has been rife as it unsettles what is supposed to be the norm. It is my life and I get to choose.

I have not lived a conventional lifestyle and so I see all sides of the coin because there are always more than two. I believe this has given me an ability to write this book with eyes wide open, sharing perspectives and experiences. I do not intend to polarise anyone, judge anyone, or shame anyone through writing this. I am not interested in being put into a box around my perspectives. I am free to write and it is time I shared what I really think. I have shut down what I witness daily as a human too often and now it is my time to speak. Ahhh, the freedom of expression ...

I hope you can read these words and make up your own mind. Take care to defend any system if you disagree but first PAUSE ... reflect and contemplate. Then make your decisions. Blame or complaining does not support your evolution.

I hope to wake up even more humans so they can see all of the options. But be aware, activating your current models is not always comfortable. What follows is an empowering you who is able to think for themselves and new beliefs that create new realities. Opening your eyes is required.

Fear is not helpful to us as a race, it disables us. We have had enough of fear, we want a new way of being human. I hear this from you and I am listening.

May it serve you like it has me. May you reinvent yourself with powerful new decisions that align to new paradigms that will serve a new reality for you. The hamster wheel is not an option. Repeated suffering is not necessary.

You are important. You story does not need to match mine. It is all relative.

I just spoke to a friend and she was downloading the intensity of her past year. She was minimising it, making it insignificant. We changed that fast! And then released it so she can get on with her healing.

A technique we use often to accelerate reinvention.

From my heart to yours, I wish for you an extraordinary life, one that is blessed with depths of human realities but coupled with stunning moments of love, joy, and expansion.

This is my wish for you.
I hope we may meet soon.
Love freely,
Mia x x x

# CONTENTS

# CHAPTER 1

# A NEW TYPE OF SUPERHERO

"*I have lived the ultimate life as a human being, yet no different to many. I have survived much pain, loss, trauma, and heartbreak. Some say my life has been extreme and one of a superwoman. To me, I am as human as they come. I get smashed to the ground and I get back up. Perhaps that is the only difference is I refuse to allow these setbacks to break me or keep me small. I will continue to go on even on the darkest days. Being human is far harder than I expected and yet bursting with richness too!*"

*MIA MUNRO*

I was born into a beautiful family in the small yet rich country of New Zealand. I spent many years travelling with Mum to the Pacific Islands for her work and was exposed to many interesting realities.

Life has been as complex as it has been beautiful. I have always been too emotional, too sensitive, and too much for many. I have struggled with not feeling like I fitted in and often been in an observer role watching the people around me do their thing. And to be honest, this thing called being human has never made sense to me. I had a big spirit as a child and an exquisite mind. A huge heart and a determination to have a wonderful life.

When my dad, suddenly died when I was 15 years old I was shattered and the moment of hearing he had passed was a moment I will never forget. The shock was so huge; there was so much I never got to say to him. But even back then I coped and looked to the positives that I was living with my mum so that gave me some security. But loss is loss. I didn't get to process that grief much at that stage and so it was destined to emerge later in life. I feel like I hardly had a chance to know him.

I grew up as the youngest of four in the family until Mum remarried and we became a blended family of six. My role was clear: it was to look after my sister, who had an intellectual disability, stay out of trouble, and be kind. I played this role well but it wasn't an easy one to play. My brothers did boy things like burning down the back of the house, stealing, and smoking; I stayed good to please my mum. The pleaser in me developed extensively to my detriment over the years.

Life was sweet; my parents were kind and encouraged us to think for ourselves. Our upbringing was in the outdoors and life experiences were our best education. We travelled lots and we moved a lot. I feel very lucky for that upbringing.

At age 45 I had lived in over 52 houses, so moving was kind of the norm, something I try to minimise these days.

Allow me to share some of my stories so I can begin to bring reinvention into reality for you.

## The Adventure Calls

*"I hear the call and I'm ready, I want to see the world beyond this country"*

Growing up I had this intense drive, especially after Dad died, to live fully. I kind of knew that life could be taken away from us at any time so I made big decisions fast and have done so many exciting things that many dream of. Many came with a cost but I always saw the benefit in the big and exciting adventures. I love adventure, like jumping out of planes, bungy jumping, cage diving with great whites, swimming with whales, spontaneous trips around the globe, and so much more. I have always been a risk taker, never knew it any other way.

I travelled to many countries at a young age. I decided to become an ambassador of New Zealand at age 16 after losing my dad and went on a student exchange to Argentina. I attended a Spanish-speaking school and rapidly learnt to speak the language. The culture shock was enormous. I went away overseas as a shy young girl who felt culture shock, fear, and was so out of my comfort zone and returned a stronger, more self-aware young woman. I was exposed to some crazy things in Argentina which created more fear than I admitted until later in life.

After graduating from nursing school in Wellington, New Zealand, I left for London for several years and worked as a nurse. I attended many hospitals and my learning was on a speedy pace as I was thrown into new hospitals and environments as a casual nurse.

I applied for nursing worldwide out of London and the call came very quickly to decide if I wanted to go to USA, Portugal, or Zambia. Where was Zambia? I asked. Ha! I had no idea it was an underdeveloped part of Africa. Sounded fun! I certainly was not prepared to arrive to a farm in the middle of nowhere with no electricity. My job was to nurse the son of a wealthy Zambian family who was dying of melanoma in his final stages of life.

My plane was delayed in London and I anxiously awaited the call to hear how he was. Upon my arrival I was given the news that he had passed over while I was in the air, so I arrived to a different situation than I had expected. I felt so uncomfortable to arrive to a grieving family in a foreign country. I was only in my early 20s. I stayed on at the farm and did some grief counselling with the family. They were determined for me to see some of Africa in my remaining weeks so I was welcomed to stay on at their other beautiful farm. The most generous people!

After a big day enjoying their lifestyle, which consisted of walking around a large farm that held a commune of around 100 workers who looked after the land, I headed to bed, exhausted. It had been emotionally draining doing grief counselling, and I struggled with the heat and being in a foreign country.

In the middle of the night I woke abruptly, a little disoriented about where I was, to a loud sound of a gong. The farmer of the house called me to get up and help him.

We jumped in the back of a truck and headed up the dry dirt road. I was hardly awake but could sense an emergency on our hands.

As we arrived, the farmer instructed me to go inside. It was steamy hot and the candlelight did little to help me see who was inside the mud hut. I strained to see and was really afraid of what we were to find.

In the corner of the hut was a young girl around 16 years old with a very big belly. She was pregnant and she was not happy. The father of her baby was in another hut that night with another mate, a common occurrence in that commune. I felt angry and was shocked to hear this. But who was I to project my view on people from a completely different culture?

I never expected to be asked to deliver my first baby that night. Wow, what an eye-opener. I had been a nurse out of training all of 18 months! I was handed gloves and I double gloved because of the risk of HIV in that commune. Lucky I had read the chapter on delivering babies in my nursing training. But to be honest, I had no idea! The farmer knew more than me!

The labour was long and the young girl struggled so much. After many hours I was able to catch her little baby girl and cut the cord and tie it with some old string. She went on to have complications and I had to stop her haemorrhaging manually, which thankfully we did. A very confronting situation for both of us. This was a life-changing experience and one that helped me grow up rather rapidly! It shattered many of my beliefs about the way things should be according to my Western societal upbringing.

The next day I returned with her to the town a few hours away on the back of the truck to ensure Mum and baby were fine. The truck was dusty and it was so smelly and humid. The potholes were uncomfortable and the journey slow. But we didn't complain. When I heard the news that the little baby was to be named Mia, I was deeply moved. This is something I will always treasure. I often say I left a part of my heart in Africa and am yet to return. But I will. This was a significant stage of reinvention for me. I was so naive.

I moved to Australia at 24 years old and worked in a private hospital in Melbourne. I moved through the ranks quickly but began to lose faith in the health system rapidly. My naivety left me after London and I saw so much of what was really happening in a system that was supposed to be about health. After seeing the risks nurses were placed under and a system that did not really protect them I moved to the pharmaceutical industry.

I knew I was going to build my own business one day so I felt that being trained in that industry would serve me long term. And it indeed did teach me business. But not always the good parts about business. My eyes were opened to a corrupt system where we were used as representatives to sell drugs, many of which were causing more symptoms and issues than good. But I was naive in my first years until I started to uncover the truth.

After being accused of "brass plating," which was proved to be not true, and outing a corrupt commission system, I resigned and was given a lovely covered-up exit. The threats from management were so hard to stomach and this became my first real case of bullying. Seeing the greed around business made me feel sick to my stomach and this was to be the beginning of witnessing so much more. I was veering on a path that was unconventional and I began to feel isolated from my peers.

I had to be free of the lies, bullying, and control tactics that corporations were using; if I had stayed in that industry I would have lost my soul! I nearly did.

At this point I was called to a new adventure, one of running my own business on my own terms! Woohoo! I fantasised about being a self-employed business owner. I dreamed of sleep-ins and no time clocks. I saw money flowing in abundance to me, whilst sunning myself on sun loungers. I imagined four-hour work days. Oh, the delusions we are sold!

A new stage of reinvention was to begin but one that was rather unconscious resulting in hard work that required a fighting spirit.

I was clear that I had to follow my truth, but little did I know how turbulent this journey would become. I had many days regretting waking up to truth. I wished I was asleep and in a daze, to avoid seeing what was happening around me. But this was not to be; as life went on I saw more and more. Some things were so hard to digest. I didn't want to be part of the human race anymore. I began to reject systems, greed, and control. The rebel was emerging! I chose to turn away from being human and escape as best I could through distractions like alcohol, frivolous parties, and spiritual practices. This was never to be the solution but I did have a lot of fun along the way.

I knew I was not a follower, it was not in my make-up. I was to become a leader, even if I wanted to hide away; it called me daily. I recognised that I had many trials to overcome (don't we all) to have the capacity to walk this path fully. Reinvention would become my daily process. It was that or give up to a system that would kill my spirit.

My only question: how will I thrive as a human in a corrupt world full of deception and delusion? I was so young and the thought of another 50 years pretending not to see what was going on felt like a death sentence. It can be overwhelming to see everything so clearly and not be able to do anything.

# Do I Really Want This Adventure?

*"Bold moves to change my mindset comes with a greater need for courage"*

It became clear that I chose to walk the plank, ha! I mean, walk the path from employee to self-employed: I started to see the craziness of those who chose the path of creating their own business, becoming an entrepreneur and leading their own life. It looked so sexy when the wealth mentors spoke about it from stages so we would buy their programmes. But the reality is often far from it. From one chaotic reality to another! Getting used to irregular income, the realities of the aloneness of working for yourself, the energy drain, the self-motivation required, and working from home began to take its toll.

The temptation to take on employment again and join the mainstream way of life started to draw me back in. I felt alone, scared, and uneducated! Did I really have it in me to take on what seemed a radical trust game of self-expression and self-reliance?

I sat in hours of fear and uncertainty. I knew I wanted a new way of being and creating income but I had no idea how. Would it be worth the journey, long hours, and pure fear at times? Would I go deep into debt? Would I ever be successful and did I have what it takes? All those common doubts I am sure you have considered yourself.

# Meeting My Guides

*"When we are ready we call in the mentors to guide us"*

I wrote my first book to capture my thoughts called *Get Real: Why Wouldn't You?* which is on Amazon. I was naive but ready to express myself. I often reread it to remember my thought processes back then. I did go on to distribute 3000 copies over a few years but I had no idea what I was doing! "Fake it till you make it" was the statement of one mentor back then. That never really sat with me. The book did go on to open many hearts. I received beautiful messages about it and still do years later. It was from an innocent perspective, way before I really woke up!

I was in Brisbane, Australia when the call came to go to a big event with a guy called Chris Howard. I knew I needed to go and this was a major turning point. I was angry, hurt, and lost with a massive vision beyond my understanding of how my life would become!

I was apprehensive at first, it all seemed too much and hyped up but I trusted as much as I could and had no idea what was yet to come. I was called up on stage and after a process it was like the light came on. The trauma unlocked and the student was ready!

What was to come was beyond my comprehension: I felt ripped open, challenged to my core, and my beliefs shattered into pieces. I wanted to run many times, but my soul knew this was the preparation for the big game of life I was choosing. Chris's work transformed me from a lost and angry gal to a strong and opinionated woman with a purpose. And later in the journey I was able to see Chris as a peer. I respect his business growth coupled with great challenges, he is human after all. I would always be grateful to him and his work.

I toured Australia, New Zealand, and the UK supporting his work and learning the ropes. This became a blueprint for my own tours and opened up my expression for my own work. For this I am grateful.

But there came a time to break free; his ship was sinking and I needed to uplevel and reinvent myself beyond his teachings. I experienced much bullying from some of his trainers (I still do not know why they wasted time on little me) and lost so much of what I created through sheer hard work and focus. But of all his students I was determined not to fail. It was just a sign to reinvent myself and take on the next level.

I am so glad I got out at that time for what happened after that was so awful to witness. The mentor was pulled under, the trainers who had been given entire careers turned on him. I witnessed the darkness of humans, but luckily from afar. This was something I was to experience as I also grew to new heights later in life.

## The First Milestone

*"Leaving the old to embrace the new. The steps are unknown"*

When I knew it was time to leave that sinking ship, I had a new challenge ahead to find my own feet and belief in myself. I had lost some through those experiences. What was the truth of what I really needed? I needed to remove the masculine programme and much of the programming to find my uniqueness again. Some of the programmes I had taken on were not to serve my next chapter.

I turned inwards to my soul and began listening to spirit. The voice I had heard at three years old. My god, my inner knowing, and my guide. I had rejected this so many times but it was the only way forward. I had lost so much faith in humanity.

11

I felt lost and alone after leaving that community as I had given my all to them for four years and I now had to find a new pathway. It seemed I had to experience almost a conscious turning away or rejection at each stage—not fun, very confusing and alienating.

At this point I knew there was no turning back; my connection to my truth became a fighting force for good and I started to see the darkness and the light in all.

I wrote and began talking about authenticity and recognising that this was one of my strengths. I began calling BS to so many concepts and challenging what was. I had a fire in my belly for expression. My own voice and my own philosophies began to develop but it came with more confusion. I was open to learning more but so much of the personal development world in reality just did not feel right. The conflicts in the teachings were becoming so obvious to me.

I met the next group of mentors who would teach me some of the greatest lessons yet.

The offer of investment funds to develop my wealth profiling system arrived and this would catapult my career into the stratosphere. Well, for some time anyway!

From lone wolf, I began the journey into big business with a strong investment behind me. I was on fire as I could express my entrepreneurial flair freely. Part of my genius is seeing gaps in teachings or strategies and I loved to find solutions to these problems. My energy became insanely high and I started to download wild and profound insights to industry problems.

My first project, the profiling tool, was to be used in the wealth industry and would measure attitudes around wealth creation. I loved Roger Hamilton's wealth dynamics tool for finding the path of least resistance but I saw a missing part to it. I had also seen gaps in the world of coaching. So often students would sign up for a programme and then think it was not working for them. The impatience and desire for quick fixes was becoming a block to their success. They were finding it hard to measure real change in their life or business. And often there was so much to correct in mindset and wealth skills before the change in money was evident.

They would make such major changes and as coaches we would witness these but they would struggle to see it in themselves. So we needed something to measure change in core areas. This became the MPowered Personal Profile and went on to help many people as the "Wealth Performance Profiling System."

This was during the era of modelling—not fashion modelling, but behavioural modelling for success. Anthony Robbins introduced me to this first, then Chris Howard after that, and I applied it diligently.

Modelling was incredible for some time but then a whole bunch of clones were created. Humans modelling each other, not modelling behaviours. A misguided interpretation of the concept that was being taught. We see today little mini Tony Robbins everywhere trying to be him. Wouldn't it be easier to be yourself? I had to create something moving forward. A process of moving further towards my own authentic expression of self. Individualism needed to be developed, not models of others!

Imagine a world of little clones; well, you probably do not need to imagine because they are everywhere, regurgitating the same work of early gurus. Ouch! What harm would come for the relationship with one's authentic self within this era? I always joke that it was no coincidence I lost my company only months after my mentor did. I modelled him so well! A gap in my insight, I now see.

I engaged a psychologist and using my unique ideas the MPowered profile was born. The beginning of the measurement of authenticity and congruency alongside personal responsibility and some other common concepts that would allow for a human being to begin to really connect into themselves for real success.

This took me straight on stages around Australia and New Zealand and my passion of speaking was fully birthed. With rapid success I experienced the ride of my lifetime. I was able to employ friends and step more into the CEO position. I was riding the wave and loving it. But with every big wave comes a rise and a fall until the next set of waves emerge.

## The Rise and Fall of That Huge and Glorious Wave

The exhaustion of working six days a week became evident. My private life was struggling as I had little left to give. I had attracted a guy with narcissistic behaviours who happily lived off me and I allowed it for some time until his behaviour became impossible as I uncovered his lies. A pattern I would repeat again later in my life. My naive mind caused me to have little boundaries, My dream of love was misguided.

As I became more and more exhausted my business partners wanted more and more of me and something had to crack. The next shock came after my business partners decided to commit fraud and completely wipe out a few companies in a group of which my company sat within. Overnight my creation, my baby I had built, was over. We had impacted thousands of lives and suddenly boom, it was gone! Deception was rife and I lost everything. The loss was devastating but having my friends who worked for my company lose their jobs too was the most painful of all.

It was time to assess everything—reinvention began to become more conscious here.

I needed to remove myself from my usual environment to be able to unhook myself from the way everything had been. I left the Gold Coast, Queensland. I packed up my home, stored my car with a friend, and stored basics at the house of a friend's mum.

I figured at this point I could either wallow in pain and loss or create contrast. So I booked a plane ticket to Thailand and headed away from what I knew to find what I needed most and the next-level options.

I took myself to Pattaya for a business conference which also happened to be one of the highest trafficking areas of Thailand where sex slavery was the norm, with prostitution a normal and very public activity. I had been working with Destiny Rescue who were rescuing children from sex slavery. I had visited there before with business groups, taking them through the journey of child trafficking for the purpose of seeing how their businesses could integrate giving to this cause in their business agenda.

David Cavanagh was running a conference there and welcomed me to join them for a week. He knew of my loss of company and I was so grateful to him. In my first week I attended the online marketing conference and that gave me a reference point to land in Thailand. I met some amazing people who would then become great friends.

I did however witness western men who were disgusted as I spoke about child trafficking in the daytime and then would buy prostitutes at night. 'They were adults and consented' was the common statement. Grrr, the confusion in me grew. As if any prostitute chooses that path over there. They begin as children and it's very difficult for them to leave.

After the conference was completed I decided to walk the path of waking up each morning and trusting what direction I needed to head in next. I fell into grief quickly and started to mourn the loss of my creations, my business, and the life I had created. I grieved for all the children and those in need. The street dogs and the darkness of our world.

But each evening I would go into the "walking street," the sex tourism area, and face the realities of life. It had me question my own loss and I began to heal. It gave me contrast for my own selfish reasons to heal.

I experienced far more than I ever expected.

My heart opened and I experienced the most intense pain of all the little girls, some as young as six years old. A new mission began. One that would take me deeper into pain and through into a new roller coaster ride. My life as an empath was about to be accelerated.

One evening, I sat next to a little girl; she was the younger sister of one of the dancers. She was six years old. They brought her out to sit with me. She was shaking in every cell of her body, dressed up in a bikini. I became so afraid that she would become the next one to be sold as a sex slave that night, for she was a virgin and hot property. And of course she was.

Anger rose in me ... I felt I had seen the darkest parts of humanity. I wanted to scream. I could not do anything. I cried and cried and screamed inside for this injustice. I ached for days with sadness and could not eat. I was so deeply affected that life had to take on a new light.

I knew from here on I needed to be true to myself. The world of making money for personal gain only was not a big enough reason. I needed to access my abilities to really do something profound and meaningful! I see entrepreneurs talk about charities often to make them look or feel good but to get in the trenches and really do something is where the real reinvention is accelerated. (This is not everyone's path, we all do it our own way.)

I chose from that point onwards to speak out and become an advocate for these young girls. I sponsored 10 young girls and encouraged many others to do the same. I visited the facilities of this organisation in Asia and I actively read and understood as much as the human mind can fathom about why this devastating issue of trafficking was happening.

I learned quickly the root cause of this was greed, and that it was not just the obvious countries like Thailand and Russia that this was happening in. It was a worldwide issue and undercover in most areas. It even exists right here in Australia, the country I have chosen to live in today. You can read today about the paedophile rings and links of human trafficking to the major leaders, politicians, and even worldly figures whom many of us love.

This sickened me and I became a disempowered and disgruntled activist. Hating humans for what they were doing, at times I contemplated giving up altogether on being a human in any normal form. I thought about living off grid forever and in other countries to stay away from the pain and suffering that humanity was causing. I wanted to escape reality. It seemed the easier route.

I broke into a million pieces and needed to take some time to ground and find my way back from the escape route I was envisioning. I needed to tune into my god and listen. I needed to rebuild faith; without faith I was lost.

A lovely woman Serena offered me her villa in Bali to take some downtime in while she was away and the gifts started to flood in to support this time. As throughout my whole life so far, doors have always opened from the most unlikely people at the most unlikely times. My gratitude remains high for all of those people with huge hearts! I have always been looked after, and okay in each stage. This is why I am baffled why so many people stay stuck in the matrix holding on to a false sense of security. To me that is worse, but who knows, it has not been my path.

I took on the challenge of rest time in Bali, Indonesia. This was a new concept after years of going for it with full force! This was to become a recurring challenge of a great need to rest and only one I am working on mastering now. I feel I will always be working on the master of my own energy.

## Time to Get Tested

*"Life is a series of big fat tests and it's how we overcome them that paves the way for a new future to unfold"*

Bali turned out to be a godsend for many years. And boy, was I tested at that time. My new business went wonderfully until the craziness of Bali energy entered into my sphere. I ran retreats which were always sold out and I built global leadership teams whom I loved dearly. I found deep fulfilment in this work but also met darkness in myself and others due to the rapid vibrational shake-up energy that calls people there.

But this is where I unconsciously created Mia's next version of superwoman. I began experimenting with ceremony and spirit and some whacky things happened. I went beyond my safe zone and I experienced many things that I share at my retreats these days in a more private and sacred space. Many were very unsafe experiences on reflection.

Having not taken long enough to heal fully from the exposure to the little girls being abused and the loss of business I began attracting bullies around me. I held a lack of boundaries and some crazy incidents occurred, signalling to me that I needed to go inwards again and find my peace and truth. I had to break connections with some clients and block darkness and their control.

I needed to develop a clear safety circle around me of people whom I could trust. There was so much deception, poor behaviour, and clients not paying after I fully delivered a service. It was not sustainable. The lessons were painful. I took responsibility for my part and their part at this time which I learnt later released them of taking responsibility for their own poor behaviour. So I had to disconnect from that community and start to source people more in alignment.

This stage is never fun for me! I love so deeply. It's painful to end chapters. It is also self-loving and necessary.

The superwoman positioning that I found myself in was far from serving my needs. I felt like any hint of me being human back then was met with huge criticism and the colluding amongst clients was nasty. I wanted to fall from that position but I did not know how to. I faced so many nasty people after giving my heart to so many. Human nature, I guess. My physical body started to become ill through the stress. I felt a victim of this at the time and it was very painful.

After an incredible year of touring to several countries with a wonderful group of people in our global leadership team, we were nearing the end. I needed to reset and holding the light for 12 months was again making me so very tired. I had not learnt how to manage my energy yet. And again I experienced similar backlash. By now I was beginning to understand human beings and boundaries and as I released my connection, those people exited rather rapidly, led often by the lowest vibrational person. Ahh, what a rough ride this business gig is!

At my final Bali Activation Event, when I was about to share the next year's programmes, which no doubt would have sold out, I got slammed with a loud internal message: STOP!

So I removed any sales and that was it. The end of that ride. Within months it was clear it was time to return to Australia, nearly four and a half years later. Bali had woken me up, shown me the most magnificent joy, upgraded me spiritually, and I loved deeply. It had also shown me my weaknesses face on and I knew that life back in Australia was about to take a completely new spin.

The tests of Bali were clear: I needed to slow down to speed up, I needed strong boundaries, I needed to be less accessible, and I needed major balance. I also needed to accept humans are humans. They will love you and quickly turn against you. They are fickle and look to blow you off your perch. We are surrounded by it. It was time to return home to who knows what. The unknown again and maybe a chance of a little more bliss! Please?

## Getting Close to a New Reality

*"I can see a new way in sight, I believe in the possibilities. I walk forth boldly and with courage"*

Returning to Australia came with dread, uncertainty, and confusion. I missed my family and friends but I was no longer the same woman that left after losing the business. I was still lost, had huge ascension symptoms with problems with my ears and dizziness. I had been exposed to so many tropical bugs my physical system was struggling, and I now see I had never healed the initial trauma fully; it layers upon layer as we move through life, not resolving the trauma as we go. Hence we have an angry society of human beings! Go figure!

So approaching Australia with an open heart, I made sure I was home for my mum's 70th birthday. A chance to celebrate with family and one of the best memories I have with them all together. We dressed up, played like crazy cats, and laughed and sang for hours! No dramas, just pure enjoyment! Playing dress-ups has always been like a releasing of seriousness for me. It brings out the joy in most. (Make note I must plan another one with family and friends!)

To prepare for my return I needed to reflect deeply on what my needs were, get rest and support. The solo Bali ride far from my soul sisters and family had taken its toll and now I could be home with those I loved. But to prepare them for the next version of Mia and for the changes at home was necessary.

I returned and felt I did not fit in straight away. The system seemed like the most controlled and conservative system after living in Indonesia. Integration was tough. I wanted to leave a million times but committed to riding it out. I was determined to begin to see the blessings of Australian life. I knew there were many to see.

## The Biggest Test of All

*"When faced with the loss of someone you love, you make critical decisions that shape the rest of your life"*

Just as I was settling into the Gold Coast and consulting to a wealth creation company and loving it, I faced one of the biggest tests of all.

The call from Mum, saying, "Your sister Marnie has had a heart attack. She is in hospital and I think you should come up to us on the Sunshine Coast."

I called a dear friend who arrived within hours and drove me up to my family. I had not bought a new car at this stage so this was the reality at that time. Marnie soon had several more tests and we heard that the prognosis was not great. She required open-heart surgery to survive and being a woman of 48 years old living with an intellectual disability, it was not a given that she would be allowed surgery. But we were not ready to let her go. She was my baby sister in my mind and I committed my life to serve her and be around for her. She was the reason I wanted to become successful, My Why. And here I was with the thought of losing her. I had planned to look after her if my parents passed, her and my souls were interconnected. She was my greatest teacher. She was so easy to love. A woman full of pure joy.

My mum and I stuck tightly together through this time and we became advocates for her. We confronted doctors and presented her case. She had every right to have treatment like anyone else. This was a devastating time as my sister could not understand what was going on. She could not be left alone at the hospital at night so I began the night caring role on an already depleted body. She would not take medications or often would not eat. She was distressed and confused by it all. It was hard to watch her suffer.

I had hardly had a chance to re-establish myself and I spent eight months travelling up and down the coast to be with her. I chose to be with her over building my business and new life back in Australia. I never regret this but the financial and emotional impact was significant. This was one of those fast decisions that held major consequences for me later.

I was supposed to be integrating into Australia, healing from spiritual upgrades, and I ignored it all to be with her. On Oct 11th, 2015, our special girl passed over peacefully. The battle was over for us all, after fighting for her rights, making resuscitation decisions, and, for me, spending nights in hospital so she was safe.

A devastating moment in our lives as many humans faced the loss of someone who brought such joy. I wondered if I would ever feel joy again like I did with her.

The grief was real, the major crashing waves and then the more subtle ones. Over and over, it seemed to take years to overcome. I lost my purpose for some time.

This book was handed to the publisher on 11th October 2019, exactly 4 years after she passed. Sacred and symbolic for me of my radical reinvention. The establishment of my own joy deep within.

Being the superwoman who had finally removed my superwoman cloak, I chose a new partnership in a business based in Sydney. I thought I had lost so much time and so went for it: no small feat to step into a major role in taking a group of 43 high-net-worth entrepreneurs off to the Amazon and Rio De Janeiro just weeks prior. I stepped into a chaotic situation and it was a race to get this adventure prepared for in a very limited timeframe. I focused on my excitement to escape to another country and create new experiences. I met some very special people on this trip whom I still value highly today.

But on a deeper, more human level it was a poor decision to make so soon after my sister dying as it caused me to miss all the cues and red flags that were to come. It was at this time I met the man who I allowed to enter my world and whom almost destroyed my world fully.

I missed all the red flags, the crazy stories I would normally challenge, and the stories riddled with lies and deception. I did not trust my intuition on any level. I ignored the warnings from his past partner, and the previous relationship I had been in 15 years earlier, and I headed off on my Brazil experience.

Ignoring red flags and warnings is not a smart thing to do. "No, Mia, it isn't," says my higher self! But it's what we do sometime. Life was about to get far worse before it could get better and much of it I could have avoided. Take note, we are always, I mean, always, being shown red flags or green go signs but if we choose to ignore or our ego blocks them then it results in some form of wake-up situation. The biggest lesson of all was to come. Listen to your own guidance and influence your own decisions. Take note and talk to your loved ones if you see red flags. Had I done this the next few years would have taken a different route. I do not believe one needs to go through trauma to upgrade! But it seems I did!

I returned from Brazil so depleted after experiencing the most insane dramas being created by leaders and clients and after having to manage insane and crazy situations one would never expect. Gun threats from the Mafia, aggressive members from the trips, accusations, and insane behaviour. The leader of this business's way of coping was to wipe his hands clean and throw the responsibility on me. Poor leadership that put my life in danger. Oh, what lessons, hey?

I fell into the arms of the person I knew was traumatised from his own path and who had already abused a previous wife. I had been warned. Oh Mia, seriously, you chose the rough ride. I could say I was stupid or that I held such a high belief and trust in someone until proven guilty. But I wanted to believe in something good in a time of great grief. And that type of personality was all about showing up perfect on the outside. A show no one can sustain for long. The love bombing was like a Hollywood movie and I loved it. The contrasting side was like the worst horror movie.

That choice of relationship caused even more trauma with the loss of three babies. Shortly after that the aggression emerged and reactions to everything I said became daily occurrences. He became intolerant of my grief, his reactions erratic and unstable. This escalated and I became the victim of brutal attacks. From a loving man who I adored to insane anger, he flipped out after I stood up to his antics and was removed by the police.

The loss was so hard to fathom for I loved fully despite the wounding I witnessed; I just never realised it would cause me so much pain and that I was so deeply depressed and felt trapped in the confusion of this type of behaviour. I (my ego) never wanted to associate myself with the label of "Domestic Violence," hence why I never told anyone of the previous incidents. I am lucky I was not killed but I felt like so much of me was dying.

The biggest lesson of all learnt. *"Slow down, listen, and trust"*

## Seizing the Moment

*"Time to make a big decision that will shift gears"*

After 12 months of living in fear of that person I chose to find a new space to thrive in. But it was time to take a hard look at each trauma, loss, and tough experience and see it for what it really was.

It was time to rise and reinvent beyond anything I had ever experienced before.

But to do that I had to seize the truth fully. And do it with a highly skilled team who would accelerate this journey so I could find happiness again.

# Making My Way Home

*"I see a glimpse of a new life and new business ... "*

It was time to recreate my business down the path of least resistance, so I partnered with an awesome education company and a woman in NZ to take her education out into Australia and New Zealand. This was like a breath of fresh air and gave me the space to really begin what I call "Reinvention 7.0." I collaborated with this incredible education company with absolutely brilliant marketers and began to thrive again. Ah, it felt good to serve others and work with the best.

Part of that reinvention was moving communities, closing down friendships that were not for the future chapters with love, and removing any sense of unsafety which came from that past relationship. My physical needs were screaming at me that I needed to be based in a slow and grounded energetic space, right by the ocean and in a community of people doing incredible things. A place where I could create and write this book. And prepare myself fully for the next chapter.

My wealth had crashed and I was left with $43 and debts I had been told were paid resulting in a visit Centrelink for crisis support. I was so embarrassed and felt broken. However the determination in my belly ensured this reality would not become my story and soon I escalated my income from $0 to $5k then $12k then $16k then $22k then $50k a month in only a few months. With PTSD and a depleted system too! Returning to my genius abilities was the way to realise such growth so rapidly. I had to let go of how this was to look and embrace a new pathway with new business relationships. Trusting in the new doorways that opened. It was important to stay open!

I had learnt how to do everything smarter and this became part of my evidence board of my reinvention: the ability to make a comeback grander and yet more grounded than ever!

*Ahh, to feel softness, warmth, and trust again.*

## Coming Home to a New Flow

*"I dream of coming home to a place of peacefulness where everything falls into place"*

After relocating up north to the Sunshine Coast, bliss began to creep in. I was finally where I knew I needed to be. Everything fell into place quickly and effortlessly. No pushing. I had a final eight-week tour of Australia to complete then it was time to rest! The road back to full energy however was not what I had expected. A sign of more growth to come. But a necessary chapter.

After my last event in NZ, I became very unwell suddenly. They said I was hit by a nasty virus, inflamed lungs and major fatigue. I was transported from the hospital to the hotel to rest for a week and all I wanted to do was go back home and be with my cats in my new serene home. I was so close to the end of that chapter.

I had no concept that I would now have to heal pleurisy which takes months, a crashed immune system, and herniated discs from an old injury. All flared up at once and put me in bed for nearly eight weeks. Then another eight weeks to build the energy back up!

Here I faced a deeper level of truth and one that would shape many years to come.

My Reinvention 7.0 was to be the biggest one of all!

So in following my formula to reinvent again, this time I knew I had to capture every step so as not to miss anything.

By the way, I had been writing about this process for the last 15 years as a dear friend told me to capture it; thank goodness I did.

# REINVENTION 7.0 and Beyond

*"When the pieces of the puzzle of life click into place and new experiences emerge"*

It became clear that the biggest test of all was how I navigated intense fatigue into the creation of my next stage of my business journey. I know this is a part that many of you face, for to transition when your energy is low is so very challenging.

The last test was would I listen fully to my truth, would I trust my own discernment, and would I make slower, more grounded decisions? It may sound simple now I have clarified it but the process to getting to this was winding and crazy at times.

As I rested more, I became more and more unwell. This virus was crashing my biochemistry and my genetic disposition known as the MTHFR gene was being expressed with serious undermethylation; it was in full flight. Getting out of bed became a huge effort, let alone feeding myself. The anxiety was of a high level, the fevers and nightmares scary.

I have now learnt that healing from pleurisy takes months and can flare up at any time; viruses attacking my thyroid have no cure, they say, so I may have flare-ups for years to come, and herniated discs need constant painful therapy to avoid surgery! Woohoo! Exactly what I need to fully stop and tune in deeper to my physical body than ever before. And not a belief system I am prepared to accept. I do not choose to identify with this dis-ease. I am healing it all!

Here I am in a new location away from my friends, in a stunning house surrounded by brilliant people and I can't even get out of bed.

Rest, they say! I say, how do I do that? And I know I am not the only one! How does someone rest when in pain, or exhausted, or still needing to pay bills! I hear it all the time. But rest is essential and if you do not stop you often may be stopped.

How do people take months of rest when we live in a society like ours that requires most of us to work most of the time?

I created space, a lesson I had learnt in previous moments of reinvention. I anticipated this time after touring that I needed to be in a quiet space with many healing options surrounding me. The Sunshine Coast delivered them all and much more.

I know it is not so easy for many to rest with busy families, especially if you are in an earlier version of reinvention, but I cannot stress how important it is.

## Home Sweet Home

*"I have arrived and it looks different to before, there is a strength of foundation that I enjoy. May I savour this and allow it to serve me until the next upgrade"*

As I began to unpack my reality with high truth and honesty, magical moments began to reveal themselves. I had to disrupt at times such old ingrained thinking and references. And I need to continually envision an upgraded picture to my life, relationships, and business.

Home sweet home is a beautiful existence; I feel free, loved, loving, and full of joy.

My new superhero outfit fits differently: it's lighter and more vibrant. It involves radical self-care and creates joy daily. It's full of acceptance and humility. I wake up to sunrises and sit gazing for hours at the horizon. My days are structured to suit my energy needs first and foremost. I walk to the rhythm of my own drum. I sing to music freely. Ahhh, I am home.

Stage one of the reinvention formula is critical and I was prepared to do it more honestly than ever before.

I feel like I am home to a place I recognise but yet it is so different to any other chapter. It's like taking the delicious pieces of the puzzle and reforming them to create a new one. So yummy and full of opportunities for my unique self-expression.

Stages two and three enabled me to grow the business rapidly again and gave me space to write this book for you. My community is emerging and I am loving the honesty and integrity of those around me. No more competitive or jealous personalities. No more narcissistic relationships around or people who do not respect my boundaries. Business partnerships are based on honesty and belief in what is possible. A clear structure has been created of what these stages require of me and what I require of them. An active review process.

My physical reinvention has given me a very clear energy reference point to create from and I come first. I recognise the gifts of being highly empathic and am quite introverted when I need to be. I recognise my hypersensitive system that is learning to not react to toxins or stressors (work in progress). It does not need to be hypervigilant all the time and on guard for me and I can relax often. Ah, what bliss to learn how to relax! It's far more than a massage here and there: it is a way of being every day.

I am no longer in fear of being attacked, of feeling unsafe now I see other human beings' trauma so clearly. I no longer choose to engage in anything less than truth-based relationships. I choose to bring money flow through businesses I am aligned with and people I trust who embrace integrity. I am more open-minded than ever about new opportunities.

My multiple income stream model serves me well. I love the outsourced styles and also the building of teams but in ways that support my needs. My passion for music is emerging again and I acknowledge my spiritual life which means I can self-heal whilst still aware of my human needs if I do require support. I relate to those at the beginning of their connection to something bigger than themselves too and hope they may learn to self-heal too.

My ability to expand with the reinvention formula is more sustainable and I get to choose my business schedule and always will. I believe that self-expression needs acknowledgement as much as self-love. We talk so often about loving ourselves but to express ourselves means bringing in the action energy. Wealth comes from the expression of your genius.

I am under no illusion that this is it. I am as human as they come. But I have a formula that has served each upgrade and brought me to a place where I am not controlled by the systems to the same degree or influenced so much out of fear of not fitting in or being hurt.

I hope that this book brings you an incredible journey. The rest of this book unpacks it all for you so you may expand and fuel your life and business in new ways after making conscious decisions that disrupt your current thinking.

I became the hero of my own story and I love me and that is a big shift! I hold compassion for those who hurt me through their own trauma. I also forgive myself for being so very human and causing any pain for others. But that is now complete. No looking back only celebrating this very moment in time.

May you become the hero of yours! Your story has only just begun!

# CHAPTER 2

# HOW TO DIGEST THIS BOOK

"Reinvention is a process that one cannot push, control, or command through mindset alone. It involves letting go of old paradigms, embracing new constructs, and developing a new heart-set that challenges most. We as a human race are in dire need of this deeper conscious transitional pathway. Humanity needs you to stand in your power and lead them to a new world. The old ways do not work. You must lead us forth to new ways courageously! I can say I have definitely walked this path!"

*MIA MUNRO*

Does anyone consider timelines in this exploratory journey into the parts of being human? Or do we follow trends? Do we think certain events need to happen at certain times in life or at a specific age group? Are these just limitations created by our systems to have us fit some agenda? Sure, there may be biological limitations for some but overall are we just trying to keep up with what most do? Or do we throw that away and live boldly?

Are you open-minded enough to consider the complexity of what it means to be a human being? I am fascinated by being human and my back story could go back lifetimes ...

In this book, please allow me to move through concepts that you may or may not believe in. All I ask is you stay open for *"to close one's mind is to close one's soul."* That could be disastrous!

I came into this world through two incredible human beings who were perfectly imperfect for me. Some say we choose our parents to come in through and we choose our bodies and the timing. Some say God chooses for us. A whole book could be written about this. But let's say some humans come into the world to experience one pathway and others another. I would hate you to shut down based on beliefs in the first chapter. Few of us are the same and yet we live in societies that are structured around the majority. Not much fun for those of us who have entered and chosen an unconventional pathway from day one.

So if I did choose my parents, my body, and the timing I certainly had no idea that I would be in for a ride of a lifetime. A life far from simple and full of trauma, loss, and heartbreak! But also a life full of adventure, freedom, and profound depths of experience!

Ahh, what it means to be HUMAN!

Time is as much an illusion as so many other things are; it is often more about expectations and alignment to time. But this can cause us some of the greatest traumas trying to keep up or not be left behind.

As a human being I expected to come into the world with a body that functioned perfectly; I thought if I eat all the right foods and stay positive and upbeat then I would never face illness because clearly illness was for those other types of people. The ones who abuse themselves. Hmmm … here comes one of many wake-up moments! Guess what … some of the healthiest people drop dead suddenly. Unexplained phenomena! Some humans who ingest toxins and abuse substances daily can sail through life rarely touched by this abuse. Hmm … I wonder if more is at play than blaming humans for their imperfections?

As a human I also expected to meet my soulmate, do my version of settling down (which was worldwide travel and adventures in between quality home life and an interdependent relationship!). But nope, not my path! I was to be stretched and challenged by a range of partners who taught me all about delusion, escapism, abuse, lack of boundaries, and all the other juicy things relationships teach us. Thanks to all of them, for they certainly woke me up. I have felt enormous disappointment in these men in my past but am now able to see beyond that programme and hold compassion towards them all. Their behaviours were not acceptable on any level but they were wounded and hurting deep within because no human would abuse another if they were happy, fulfilled, and in joy.

As a human I expected to be safe and live far from drama, violence, or disasters. Well, that was not my path also … I have been seriously unsafe, trusted the wrong people, and had close calls to many natural disasters. Hit by lightning, just got out of bombings, beaten up, cheated on, gangs, threats, and stalking. Even exposed to corrupt authorities … stolen intellectual property and fraud.

Ha! The day in the life of a human. I know I am not special or different to so many who would be reading this book. We all have our own version of massive expansion.

As a human I expected to be able to produce a child whenever I felt like it. Miscarriages and infertility happen to other women, not me ... hmm ... that chapter is still to be written but it has become clear that I can no longer assume any normal part of being human is on offer to me., or is it the exact opposite? Am I actually in fact so damn human, a spirit living a human experience?

So wherever the root cause of all this suffering, I am unsure it really matters. Life can sideswipe us all. An empowering focus can become "reinvention." The process of moving through it all!

Because when you recognise impermanence (nothing ever stays the same) and you realise you have no control over what comes next, you let go, and the only part you have some power over is how you choose to move through it all.

The process of moving through it all!

I figure if you can move through and lift off just as fast as you have been taken down then you can build resilience, depth, and beauty! And if I can top it all off with high doses of integrity then my future realities can only be juicy and profound.

In this book you won't hear me regurgitate teachings from gurus that have great marketing abilities. You won't hear me create concepts that cause you to blame and shame yourself even more ... You will hear insights from a visionary who has walked this path and questioned everything along the way. I am not a guru or intend to ever be put on a pedestal again for I will never live up to your expectations and criticism. I am human and humans are not perfect. And I do not choose to be a target for the darkness.

If I hear another programmed leader throw around regurgitated concepts from old paradigms or past gurus beware, for I am ready to challenge you. People do not wake up and create cancer. There are many aspects to all elements of dis-ease. Trauma sits at the root of much illness and blatant ignorance does not serve anyone. It is not kind and kindness is what people need if they are in the middle of a major upgrade. It's deeper than plant-based diets or the latest product.

The other story I want to release you from now is about this concept of excuses. Sometimes people commit but they do not follow through because the leader lacks what they need to keep a community engaged. "Go hard or go home" garbage is not allowing for a whole human experience. People get sick and have to stop committed projects. People can be affected by natural disasters and also family trauma. People can change their mind and should not be wronged for it. Just do it with integrity, is all I say. Leaders are human and guaranteed to make major mistakes, often in the public eye. Allow them to be human.

Many of these masculine constructs are causing ridiculous levels of stress for too many people. I know you want success, but you can have it in a way that is sustainable for the future. A way that aligns to your unique body, your unique mind, and amazing heart. Allow your soul to lead the way, not the pressure of society and gurus spruiking a reality that is far from where you actually are!

So work through this book, and stop and contemplate as you need to! Allow yourself to digest the stories and concepts. Try them on for yourself. Disagree if you need to. Use your own discernment, make up your own mind! It is your right to decide what you need and when.

Engage in our community if you need support and go for it 100%. Do not do this alone, there are many people who understand this journey and can support you. But I ask you to engage with awareness of your own wounding. Your own stories. Allow yourself to be open but also kind, respectful, and operate with integrity.

If your why for doing this is big enough this might just be one of the most significant transformations you have ever had. I wish that for you.

So welcome to your reinvention ... the beginning of your next chapter of life, your next business-to-change-the-world project. It all comes down to creating and making decisions from the depths of your soul!

And that is the TRUTH!

# CHAPTER 3

# REINVENTION IS INEVITABLE

*"The strongest of leaders have climbed the highest mountains, overcome the greatest storms, weathered the greatest judgement and surrendered to complete vulnerability. This prepares them for the courage required to continue to reinvent one's self. There are no shortcuts. There are profound realities to be experienced when you go through the pain to find fulfilment and joy that awaits."*

*MIA MUNRO*

Everything runs a cycle. As humans we are born, we live, and we pass over. Animals and plants run the same cycles too. Our earth is constantly changing and has numerous cycles playing out on it; the seasons, the ocean, water precipitation, the sunrise and sunset, and even more changes are becoming evident because of the impact we as humans are creating on it. But one thing I completely trust as true: reinvention is inevitable; no one gets out alive without some aspect of having to change. However, if we are not proactive or cooperate in changing with life, life will cause us to change eventually.

The key is knowing how to stay connected to what's changing so you change with it.

And to be able to stay connected to it through the ups and downs by "being present" …

You can't have knowledge of the change that is occurring or the change that may be required if you are always thinking forward to what can be, without any present awareness. Or for many looking back. By allowing presence to be activated daily, we can sense into the change much more easily. This is called "slowing down to speed up"; it's how we get in sync with the changes that are necessary so we can course correctly along the way rather than need a major upheaval event to get us up to where we need to be.

This was one of the harder lessons to both grasp and fully embody.

I lived with an invincible mentality for years. My confidence in my work life was always so strong that I believed nothing could affect it. But family illness, change of relationships, market changes, career shifts, partnership breakdowns, and economy crashes are a part of the cycle of being a human. They rarely are planned and I certainly was never prepared for them. So many of my setbacks have come from the unexpected events of life.

Being derailed over and over again. I was derailed several times and the whole build up process was enormous.

I had always thought I was on track, my ego made sure of that, and so I walked blindly into many partnerships with a positive expectation of the future. But that's what we are taught to do and those who have spent years doing personal development have positive expectations often bordering on delusional at times. The "Piscean" part of myself always believed in the ebb and flow of the river and so I often made big decisions to create fast outcomes. The result would be some incredible life experiences but on the flip side major energy collapses and extreme opposite experiences.

Do I regret this? No I don't - for 45 years this gave me an experience of many lifetimes.

Having a positive attitude without real human emotions can become delusional after time and I see examples of this same delusion daily. I do not judge it as I knew it myself but it concerns me greatly. For so many to ignore the dark side will lead to major crises and cause much more suffering than is necessary. Even intelligent, kind-hearted, and strong people can be affected. It happens all the time. Some of these people will rise and reinvent but many will choose to exit life because it is just too much.

## To Rise and Reinvent or ...

*"A financial planner is determined to stay strong through a major family dispute until it is all over, whilst suffering from severe anxiety and stress daily. Containing the pain until that magical day comes to feel it. But when will that come? This is dangerous and could result in illness; for some chronic illness"*

- Reinvention Time: We need to delve into options for the releasing of stress and trauma responses. Recreate daily schedules to enable more space for rejuvenation. Reframe the family threats and bring in a strong support team to minimise further stress. She now is able to move through each stage and begin to create new models for coping with stress.

*"A talented coach with absolute genius in her field will probably never return to it. The trauma and loss associated with a past financial loss has placed her into a holding pattern. She has chosen a radically different lifestyle which involves no real flow of money. Eventually this may cause other major issues; avoiding the healing required will cause her even more pain down the track"*

- Reinvention Time: We shine light on the past and unblock that wounding. Reviewing the past experience in new light she is able to disrupt her choices and begin to recreate her true mission in a new form. Her wealth mindset is given an upgrade and her self-worth challenged to allow for expansion. She has a new plan to double her income which will expand her children's life.

*"A nurse in her late 60s, she has worked in the same career her whole life. If her body breaks down she has nothing saved for the future, no retirement, and would become homeless. Her work has been threatened several times with little change to her future set-up. She is choosing to ignore the realities of life in the 20th century"*

- Reinvention Time: She is recognising a complacency pattern and beginning to redefine new pathways. Utilising investment funds to consider affordable housing options. She has accessed new job opportunities that allow for less physical work. She is ready for radical reinvention, step by step.

*"A business consultant who has provided the same services for years is bored, unfulfilled, and close to burnt out. He needs time out to reassess but never created investments to manage downtime periods. Although running a consistent business and receiving $150k income per annum, is beginning to want to throw it all in. Slowly the business is failing"*

- Reinvention Time: The focus for him is his lack of abundance; he now sees major blocks in his planning and vision for the future. He plans downtime overseas in Asia to allow for expanded contemplation. He is prepared to give up the business to recreate an online business option using his previous skills. We map the transition so he can see moments of certainty amongst some radical changes.

*"A real estate agent and her husband are over it. The hustle and the challenges and the constant struggles. They pack everything up to minimise their life and live it from their laptops. This wears thin with a lack of stability and they cannot see a way to find the balance. Stress begins to affect their relationship"*

- Reinvention Time: They recognise the way in which they make decisions rapidly without future consequences. They move to a new location, set up a base, and then create lots of variety within it. They engage in new ways of relating and gain support from experts.

*"A corporate high flyer has spent her years climbing the ladders in a male-dominated industry. She is exhausted and stuck as the money flows but her energy is dying each day. She no longer has time for much outside of work and children's commitments. She has dreams she may never realise"*

- Reinvention Time: She creates time out to slow down to speed up. She takes time to remember her own needs. She accesses new opportunities to begin to expand possibilities. She knows she needs to plan her transition out of corporate.

She recognises this can be a process and can strategically plan it through. She seeks guidance from those who have been there before.

We can turn against our past experiences or we can seek to become aligned to their purpose. We do get a choice! Reinvention is in your hands.

The business and employment landscape is constantly changing; nothing is guaranteed and we'd be foolish to think we are always going to be safe. We will see the rate of homelessness increase rapidly over the next few years; gosh, I nearly ended up homeless! We are seeing suicide on the increase, cancer and illness is becoming rife, and the science is all there to what will happen to our environment if we don't make changes now. But rarely are many slowing down to be able to see the realities that will derail them eventually.

I certainly do not live in that la-la land anymore. But it was a wonderful escape from reality until truth finally prevailed and derailed me so I could learn what I'm sharing now!

If reinvention is inevitable then, is there space for a formula that can help us both see the changes in real time, and know exactly what "right" action for right now to take so course corrections can occur? Yes, there is.

This is not to live in fear or anxious anticipation but to expect the unexpected and to be ready to make choices that will support you through the inevitable changes that are already happening, with a lot less suffering and devastation.

It's totally possible and it all starts with having a special kind of plan.

# CHAPTER 4

# DON'T LIE TO ME

*"When all the lies are exposed who will own the truth?"*

*MIA MUNRO*

We are a product of our environment: we know that to be true. If I had remained living in Tonga, a beautiful island in the Pacific Islands where my family brought me up for my first years, I have no doubt that my experiences would have been different to being brought up in a more developed country. I was surrounded by Tongan culture, island lifestyle, and religions. To this day I still crave the island life and have seen myself move from one paradise location to the next one freely. The Tongans say I have a Tongan heart!

I have also chosen to live in completely contrasted environments and this has built much of my open-minded philosophy on life today. So I wonder, how much are we affected by the world we grow up in and the communities we create through different stages of our life? I believe we are impacted far greater than our minds can fathom. And how does that shape us?

I studied Quantum Physics for many years in my development to become a transformational leader 15 years ago and it expanded my view of life, way beyond where most people in my community at that time could relate to. Many people in my immediate world judged my view and its fluffiness because they just could not understand this. They thought I was too free-spirited and it made them feel uncomfortable. The shaming for being so free in my thinking and intuition started very young for me and so I shut much of this down. I saw truth, things beyond the lies. I could read lies in others easily and thought perhaps it was normal to lie or create untruths. This caused me many headaches growing up until I found truth, integrity, and the courage to be the real me!

The truth is, I always saw the world in a different light to those around me in my earlier years. I seemed to be able to see past the confusion, manipulation tactics, and sheer lies at a very young age. I saw so much with clarity, it was the humans around me that confused me most as they did not seem to be able to see what I could. I have received a lot of wisdom when I have chosen to sit deep in meditation or prayer. I have spoken to God many times and he has shown me pathways. My inner conflict was always about what if I chose to walk to the beat of my drum, then what? Would it have meant being rejected by those I love? I feared this greatly.

So I created an in-between, an incredible empathic and compassionate personality that would look to seek and understand other people's point of view. I chose what I thought would be a safe pathway—little did I know that to choose a path that is not true can become far from safe.

So let's look at some realities in this crazy world of ours. The confusion is evident and we can see this in the split in our communities, between religions and cultures. It is so hard to know what is true or real. And to have our own mind view when it is being influenced so heavily from many angles.

Only recently we saw the annual climate change rallies occur again and yet our world is no closer to solutions to this. Whilst in the past few jumped on the bandwagon for this, we are seeing more people publicly support this cause. I do feel it makes people feel like they have some sort of control when they buy into something like climate change. And this is only one theme of many that we can explore.

## Red Pill or Blue Pill?

Which would you rather …?

If you've seen *The Matrix* you'll get this reference but if not, the choice in pills is the choice in knowing the whole truth, which will completely shatter everything you think you know to be true about the world you live in; or, you can choose to remain ignorant to the truth and live in a false reality, continuing to be played, lied to and manipulated so that the controlling power continues to have control over you, over what you think, your wellbeing and how you get to live your life.

Take a moment now and ask yourself. If you were given a choice, what would you rather?

Actually, let me give you a smaller metaphor that will help you make this decision on a wider world view.

What if you were in a long-term relationship with someone who you absolutely loved and adored and who acted as if they completely loved and adored you too? Someone who was also having relations with multiple other people behind your back but made you feel like you were the only one. Would you want to ignore the evidence you keep rationalising away, forgive the lies they told to explain when things didn't add up, and stay in this false reality? Or would you want to know the truth so you could make better decisions for yourself?

Most people choose to stay in the false reality. Why? Because it's easier to believe that you already know the truth, that everyone is who they say they are and are doing what they say they're doing or not doing. That there is no big bad in the world and everything ends like a Hollywood rom-com movie. Wouldn't that be so lovely?

Those who choose truth, those who choose to see through the false reality and who choose to no longer be manipulated by the narrative, choose the harder path. Why? Because they are going against the grain, against the mainstream masses, and against those in power who are trying to keep control of them. It takes courage to sit in this position.

Guess what happens to the people who choose to know the truth though? They not only dare to see it but they are willing to accept the evidence that it's real, and then many also feel the need to speak about the truth so others can know it too. What happens when they do that? People call them "conspiracy nuts" even when the evidence is there if they are open to looking at it. But that's the problem: their mind is already shut.

So basically you're either ignorant and a sheep, or a conspiracy nut. There's not much in between. Really?

I'm not here today to dive into conspiracy theories where people are being controlled and manipulated, that's a much bigger conversation and not entirely the point anyway. I'm here to trigger you to open your mind and think for yourself. And dare to face the truth and open to the real world you live in.

Open your mind to look at the real evidence around you, evidence that things aren't as they seem. This is not about becoming paranoid and believing everyone is out to get you because that's not true either, that is just the opposite extreme. It's about being objective even when it goes against the narrative in your mind and against the narrative of those around you.

When you dare to unplug from false realities, and I'm talking about the false realities in every area of your life including the false realities you have created within yourself, then you are finally in a position of power in your life. No one is in their power while they are being controlled by someone or something outside of them. No one is in power when they are operating on assumptions that are just regurgitated programming repeated by the masses.

When you are able to see the full truth then you are able to make much better decisions. You are able to define who you really want to be, what your life is going to look like, and how you are going to get there, but also when you do this, you will know what the real game board of life looks like so you can set yourself up to win personally, as a community and as a united world.

This is a big part of reinvention. Daring to see and know the truth. Daring to be objective and look at the evidence to make up your own mind, and disrupting the narrative that's being fed to you. It's time for the world, our communities, and each individual within them to reinvent themselves so we can move into a new and much better way of living, loving, and supporting each other to thrive abundantly together.

Let's imagine it's true that we are being fed a whole strategic series of untruths? What if the very thing you are rallying for is exactly what the powers that be wish for you to rally for? What if you are being distracted from what is actually happening? What if weather engineering for example is in fact real and our environment is being controlled, much like every part of being human? My choice or view is irrelevant here; my role is to present a picture which might activate you to slow down and consider what you personally think, rather than continue on the follower journey. Empowerment comes from creating your own pathway and more and more of us have chosen this path. It comes with both exciting moments and different types of stress.

The challenge with taking on radical beliefs about something in order to activate change is we can often plummet into devastation and destruction. So much so that it overwhelms us on many levels, so we either at this stage decide to conform or choose to block any form of truth. And when we block, that is a form of disconnection which causes other issues in our communities. Communities full of loud activists who polarise others or silent disconnected humans. Not really living a whole human experience.

How do we exist and even reinvent ourselves in an ever-changing world that is so difficult to grasp? Well, only you can answer that for yourself. What we do know is this: much of what we believe to be real is not. We do need to try and see the forest through the trees. But we could spend our time worrying about so much out there instead of focusing on what is of most critical importance, and that is YOU! Your life and your choices.

Our world will continue to change and we will see major crises ahead of us. But we cannot live in fear of these for to do so will not create harmony, joy, and love which are essential ingredients for your own personal happiness!

What you can decide on is how you choose to interact with the world you live in. The country you choose to live in, the vibrational engagement, and the philosophies that will support your success. It is up to you!

## Let's Look at This From a Global Perspective— What Is Happening Out There?

"He who manipulates the words and provides evidence best, wins the ears of the ignorant."

Is it true that money controls people, people determine truth, but truth is manipulated? So what is real in this world of ours? The truth is that nothing is as it seems.

## Wealth—Our World Is Controlled by Evil People Who Need Power to Survive!

What do you think immediately when you read this statement? Do you believe this to be true or does your mind prefer to believe that we are surrounded by love and light? What is your version and do you actively choose to believe that or was it an automatic programme based on your environment?

Growing up I have seen it all. The darkness, the light, and everything in between. But it was so often rejected by those around me to consider anything less than a positive view. So I chose a default pattern of seeing the good in everything. Be good, do good, and everything will be good. Ha! What a delusion that was. But I felt it would keep me safe and included so I fiercely believed it. As I grew up I witnessed so much darkness in others. At a young age, like many children, I created a fantasy world as my reference point to dissociate to when I needed to escape reality. And it served me well into my 40s when it was shattered so dramatically that I felt forced to re-evaluate this belief system and start getting real! A more balanced view of being human came next.

This process from dark to light was a deeply disturbing process which has allowed me to release trauma from years back. I nearly didn't make it through that one: facing demons, darkness, and the loss of hope for humanity was rough. But it was necessary to break down the BS I had conformed to. Can you relate? Can you see the chaos and darkness around you?

What I have witnessed, especially recently through my own shake-up, is that our government systems are not exactly supporting us to live a balanced view of life. In fact we are being manipulated through many channels and controlled resulting in more power and more money to the people at the top!

Who are the people at the top, you ask? The powerful people in our world who sit at the top of the chain controlling money, running paedophile rings, and trafficking innocent children, just to start with. The ones who will happily instruct bombs and wars to occur and kill innocent people, all in vain. Many act as politicians and leaders of major causes. Some of them I personally have even championed in my speeches over the years and given kudos to, only to find that they were even trafficking children under the guise of orphanages. Some of them have been awarded peace prizes and some are still advocating for peace and love when in fact they are directly linked to those causing the destruction.

"They are not the authority you think they are."

I do not wish to enter into thoughts around conspiracy theories, that is not my mission. I will not disclose my own views fully here, I get what's going on and I do not choose to become a target to anyone's need for more power. So I simply wish to say boldly it's time to consider who is doing what and why. It is a hard world to live in when you see the truth and even a little author like me needs to be cautious.

Not for fear reasons but for longevity of sharing my message. I see the Netflix documentaries being removed when truth is spoken; I see people disappear and I know of the threats. They are real and it will not serve our mission to reinvent ourselves if we become obsessed with them. It would be powerful if you become committed to your new life or business and how it can roll out to create a life that you deserve.

On the other side of this control tower of leaders, there are people at the forefront of our media channels or even part of major organisations that have the most stunning hearts and best of intentions. They are being used as communicators of messages to create fear in us and to also polarise us. The sad part is few are communicating the messages we really need to hear! What they are really doing and why! They are often being puppets for the agenda of others.

So why is this relevant to us? It is hard to know when we are being manipulated, when all the right words are being communicated to us. So no blame is placed on our race here. But we do now have a choice and that is in how we choose to live our own lives. We need to listen and observe more. We need to make decisions in new ways and we need to consider new perspectives.

This book is not about the power people, this is about you, so I choose to bring no more energy to them as that does not strengthen our case or deliver us what we need most. What we need is to wake up and begin to question more. That will strengthen the human race immediately. When we wake up we become powerful. But it will take some reinvention within to allow yourself to see your version of your truth. As I have discovered mine, my inner strength has grown exponentially, giving me the self-permission to even publish a book like this and return to my expression through music.

## Health—We Are Killing Ourselves, Humans Are Dying and Becoming Disempowered

What do you think immediately when you read this statement? Do you have strong opinions on this topic? Did they come from research or personal experience? Or were you told about these?

When it comes to the topic of health in a global sense it is devastating to know and understand the depth of abuse that is being created to seek more wealth for those in power. I know this is such a controversial topic to discuss and one that separates and segregates community. Too many people are following the fear-driven campaigns with a non-educated mind.

To understand the disease-driven reality we face you need to understand a little about pharmaceuticals and medicine. Here I will touch on certain themes knowing you can go and be fully educated yourself if you choose. I only choose themes I can speak about from a real human experience rather than what we are being fed through media channels.

My first career was as a nurse; I wanted to help people, just like my mum. I studied in Wellington, New Zealand and was a deeply passionate young woman on a mission to heal all! After graduating I moved to the UK to do three years of nursing in some of the finest hospitals and also Accident and Emergency settings in low socioeconomic environments. I tended to private wealthy people in their homes and was paid large sums of money to play the role of a private nurse. Often for an elderly person with little illness I would be paid to wear the lovely winter red coat shopping—a status symbol for all to see. This seemed insane to me.

I jumped into this career with enormous drive and passion, happily giving life-saving medications and treatments to those in need. The most rewarding role to play when a person is in need.

As my experience grew in this field I worked in haematology and oncology units (cancer) in London and my inquisitive mind started to take note of the patients who were administered aggressive chemotherapy and then went home finally in remission. I would then see them come back within three years with another type of cancer. Little changed in their lives and the pattern continued. The pharmaceutical drugs killed the cancer and all the good stuff too, leaving their immunity low and struggling. Rarely was self-healing a part of their prescription.

I started to question everything. After I moved to Melbourne, Australia to work in a private medical unit I started to see trends of medical patients come in so unwell then leave for home stabilised, only to return again. We loaded them up with medications and they left with many too. Nothing in their life ever really changed. The "root cause" of the illness was not our priority, we were told; just treat symptoms and stabilise and get them home. This was the main focus.

But when I joined a pharmaceutical company, I had convinced myself that I was doing good by selling a drug that I believed to be ethical. Over the five years I witnessed so much and if not for the contract we signed to not disclose any information, I would have many stories to tell.

They loved nurses as we had already been trained in giving medications without too much challenge so we would happily entice doctors through expensive lunches to use our drugs. Of course this was tightened down over the years and we just did it in different ways. Same principle.

When I was a sales representative I came across one drug that ended up being taken down due to the death of patients who had taken it. Gosh, I had even taken it and given it to my mum. Oops! I started to get really nervous of the industry and company. We went into lockdown and it was all over the media. We were instructed to read scripts to GPs and manage the panic. I knew something was wrong. But I was hooked too: I drove an expensive car for that stage of my life and was paid handsomely at the time. The perks of all-paid-for, expensive conferences kept us distracted too.

I saw so much false information. I uncovered commission schemes that were scamming the sales team and after they saw that I was perhaps someone who could see what was really going on I was taken into a big boardroom and accused of "brass plating" when I in fact did exactly what I had been educated to do. Unbelievable.

I proved my innocence and knew it was management who became threatened by me, and chose to leave on my own terms. The company and I celebrated my exit and my new career started. This was my first real experience of bullying and the power of deception.

The problem is this: if you believe in the topic of pharmaceuticals or not. Even vaccines. It is wise to know that powerful leaders out there need to find and create diseases to keep the pharmaceuticals in creation for the next big thing. I have no doubt that many drugs have helped many people. And I am grateful for the life-saving procedures that extend lives. I hold a very grounded and balanced view as I have worked in ICU and trauma units and I have saved lives too.

But when diseases are renamed in order to scare people into taking a vaccine I draw the line. I have witnessed babies nearly die post vaccine, I have seen the disorders in children pumped up with high vaccine schedules, and I have witnessed my own reactions to them … So I don't need to be an expert to know something fishy is up! This is no theory, I have seen it with my own eyes.

Some believe that diseases are created to provide a need for a vaccine. This brings in more money for drug companies. Then vaccines create side effects in the body which keeps medical practitioners in work prescribing the symptomatic relief. Then of course the companies create new drugs to manage the symptoms. More money is made and so on.

So how do they drive sales? They use the media and present scare campaigns, sales go up, we have more followers, and then more drugs need to be created for secondary conditions. A perfect sales and marketing model!

Then let's put a government behind it and start to control what our children have to have to be able to attend schools. That way they control our future generations. Kinda sick, if you ask me. But you make your own mind up. It is super important you use your discernment.

The evidence is out: we know that the current vaccine schedule is causing some very concerning side effects in little babies and children; we know the schedule is too intense and we have no control over it if we choose to have our children in mainstream education. The control is on all levels.

Another angle, just to get you thinking. Our water is pumped full of fluoride which is a highly toxic agent. Our health departments even put out claims that it is good for us. The research is there if you are curious. I removed all fluoride and experienced detox symptoms on many occasions. However, the scare tactics have created a booming water bottle industry out of fear and much of the water we buy is often not much healthier for us to ingest. Water filters have stepped in and many hold strong claims but also many do not cover the toxic metal issues we face or remove fluoride effectively! It is so confusing to begin trying to understand what is true and good for us and so for many conformity is an easier pathway.

The world of natural therapies is growing at such a rate that now the medical system funded by pharmaceutical companies is freaking out. In our natural therapy industry, doctors are being suspended for healing unhealable conditions! There are battles everywhere and we are in the middle of it. And don't tell me that this would not cause us humans added stress!

I was in South Africa many years ago, I will not disclose where or when as it was an undercover opportunity for me to witness the healing of multiple diseases with a type of oxygen infusion directly into the veins. I myself as a young nurse went into the hidden clinic and received this treatment myself. Prior to that they would say it would kill you to have this injected, but I am still alive and kicking today. Whilst doing research for this book I googled the words "oxygen 4" and within 30 seconds it said my Mac was now infected with a virus. Interesting!

So the control is real and they begin by restricting access to natural services and remedies.

CBD oil as we know has powerful healing effects and its efficacy has been proven and yet here in Australia it is illegal at print of this book. I hold a high belief this will change. I personally know of the effects of it. It is the very substance my body needed to heal. Why are incredible healing substances illegal when they are so accessible in other countries.

IV Vitamin C infusions are one of the only infusions that can turn off some autoimmune diseases and cost $200 a pop. I do them as they have been shown to reverse some viral strains. But the system do not cover this for me, instead they will give me pharmaceutical products that are not effective.

Redox supplements are powerful, they literally turn on cell signal, which means it turns on every single process in every living cell. The supplements empower the most basic building blocks in the body to thrive. I felt my energy lift as soon as I began taking them on tour.

They represent a new version of technology. Redox stands for Reductant and Oxidative. This is also something I need to fund myself. It has been life changing these 3 options.

In the world that we live in today, our cells are being challenged all the time, whether it's through the air that we breathe, the food that we eat, physical exertion, stress, ageing, we all face these challenges. We need something to help our cells function at the optimal level.

It's been scientifically shown to turn on genetic activity at the foundational level in the body in five key areas of health: the immune system, inflammatory response, cardiovascular health, digestive health, and hormone balance. It's like we are turning on a light switch in the body! It's a game changer!

But only those with open minds and money to fund these can often access these specialised treatments. If I walked the medical path I would be living with an autoimmune disease as a label and probably never get well and that was not an option!

My recent physical reinvention has involved me working with a regenerative doctor (who embraces a holistic approach) to find the root cause of my fatigue, swelling, and immunity issues. It has cost over $6k in eight weeks because not one medicine is pharmaceutically based, therefore they are not covered by the medical system which I pay taxes for! I can access IV Vitamin C at my own cost. Most people I know would not be able to afford the treatment plan I am engaging in. I pay taxes and yet I am not supported in getting well in this country! This is concerning. And to fight it seems pointless and would result in more stress. Instead my choice is to find a pathway to suit my needs and stay focused on those. I know so many walking this path. It only brings us closer to self-healing and empowerment anyway!

So whatever you choose to believe just question yourself and open your mind because media and our system are working hard to fool you. We do not need to live in a fear-based model at all! Bliss is yours, you get to decide and choose. But open your mind as there is much that is not what it seems.

*"I do not choose to be an activist in any of this, I will not be put into a box around this or shamed for my insights. I will question and make decisions based on my own discernment. I value the medical system for what it was created for. For emergency situations it has been necessary. I will embrace the natural body's healing system to create daily wellness and healing ongoing. And that is my choice!"*

It does make me gasp whenever I have had to visit someone in the hospital or even presented myself, and the nutrition available, or lack of it, is incredible for 2019! We all talk about hospital food and how horrendous it is. Many of my issues with inflammation have been toxin or allergy related so when I go in for a test or post procedure they serve me white bread with cheese in it. The rate of gluten and dairy intolerance is on the rise so why feed most people these toxins when they are trying to get well? They might as well serve a glass of bubbles with it! To someone who reacts to every part of it is not fun at all!

In Brisbane recently, I was in awe of the hospital where my stepdad was admitted for open heart surgery as he was presented with a menu to order his own food and it was balanced and healthy. Yay for positive developments! May there be more!

## Self—We Are Brainwashed and Disconnected

What do you think immediately when you read this statement? Do you often feel confused or unsure of what to believe? Do you find yourself following the masses or heavily engaged in TV and even getting caught up in the drama and hype of it? Do you often watch TV and feel worse than you did before? Do you get stuck on social media fighting for something just because?

I know we think we are an intelligent species and of course we are but we may be being controlled on many levels. We are being followed, tracked, and monitored in many ways. And no, I am not paranoid or choosing fear around this. It is what it is.

I was watching a movie on Netflix the other night and a character talked about a particular brand of baby stroller. My computer was on, my phone active, and by the next morning I was being advised on google and Facebook about buying baby strollers. It was so damn obvious! I don't even have a baby and I have never heard of that brand and yet it was being shown to me.

Go figure!

We do not get to determine our own truth much if we are plugged into the matrix. We are fed stories and only if we have developed our own intuition or done major research do we know what we perceive to be true.

Our behaviours are being watched, we are researched like lab rats and trialled on many things. And I can feel when I get affected by it. Because I suddenly feel a sense of dread in my gut. Sometimes after no exposure. So little ol' me decided to get off mainstream media, much to the disgust of my parents who still don't get me or why I would not want to tune into the 6 p.m. news every night, with its doom and gloom. You see, I don't choose to be fed the dread and BS of the news. They make up stories, hype up stories, lie, and hurt people. We know this to be true but we don't want to admit it. It's what our parents did so it's what we do.

God forbid I miss a news event! It made me chuckle many years ago when my mum said, "But what if there is an earthquake when you're on holiday in Bali and you don't know about it?"

Hehe ... brainwashed to be dependent on the news so they can ensure you stay in lack, fear, and disempowerment. Ahh, no thanks! "I think I would feel the earthquake," I replied.

On a global perspective media is being blocked! Only a few weeks back there were major floods overseas but media blocked it here. Why would they do that? The Amazon jungle begins to burn down and it takes days to hear about it. It's overwhelming to see just how much is being manipulated. Our role is to just stay open and in our hearts to what is real and what is not. We need to reduce stress and this is one constructive way to begin.

After all, we do everything in life to experience love, happiness, and joy ultimately, right? Nearly every dying man's last words were, "I wish I had spent more time being happy! Being with those I love and enjoying my life!" You have a choice; despite the way this world is going we can build our own ship!

## The Good News!

*"The good news is we are seeing some emerging trends that support the reinvention of humans. We are waking up and we are commanding new ways. Although we have a long way to go we can draw strength and confidence in some amazing initiatives and systems being built to support us as we become more empowered"*

1. We are moving away from the authoritative narrative. We are waking up to what is happening and beginning to make our own decisions. This will create empowerment amongst us. We need to listen to people and their truth with an open mind. Begin to practise using discernment, not regurgitating the same dialogue. We often do not open up as we find the reality too scary, too overwhelming, and too unstable for our mind to handle. Hence many open and shut down again. I don't blame you for that, I did for many years, but it doesn't help you navigate a peaceful and happy life.

   If you do not know what is true for you, take space and reflect with the question—"WHAT IF?"

2. People are moving away from accepting the vaccine schedules for newborn babies and young children. They are researching and questioning, making instead informed decisions. Some will continue to vaccinate, some won't, and some only partially. It's their choice and as long as they have found their own way through being informed. We are seeing many new natural health services emerge and we are trying them and seeing profound results. We are becoming more informed and wellness conscious rather than being active in a health system that does not cause health. We are beginning

to avoid hospitals unless an emergency situation to minimise the need for detoxification of the drugs used. Hospitals are providing healthier options for staff and patients. Yes!

3. We are choosing to remove ourselves from channels that feed us lies, like mainstream media. The recent fires in Queensland, Australia was such an example of the media games and hype caused to create drama. Much was misreported and spread even by locals themselves. A culture of panic and fear was evident but we are seeing people say STOP IT! We are seeing organisations work together through crises. I noticed how I only listened to Queensland fire rescue and their chosen ABC news reporter and we got a clear and non-panicked story so we could take action with ease. It was impressive.

## Let's Look at This From a Community Perspective—What Is Happening Around Us?

*"We are prevented from tapping into the true power and support of community"*

It is true that people are encouraged to compete for what they need; competition leads to separation and separation leads to isolation.

What is working in the structure of our communities? Do they serve our real needs for connection, support, and growth?

The very structure of community is meant to be designed to have us look after each other. In my experience this can and does exist but it is not the norm in many Western societies. Hence we hear so many comments of amazement when communities bind together post crises like fires, flood, or earthquakes, but we are not seeing communities look after those suffering from financial burdens or mental illnesses, for example. They are so often isolated in the desire for a perfect world full of positivity. The truth is, where there is light there is dark; it's equilibrium, so to discard and exclude those in need serves no community and yet we still exist with status levels dictated by wealth.

The flow of our working lives in today's world is becoming even crazier to sustain causing greater experiences of stress, mental struggles, and stress-related illnesses for so many. Here is the cycle for those who work as employees. You work long hours to elevate up the success ladder or longer hours to increase your income. This requires more time away from home, your family, or loved ones. To maintain the cost of living in high employment areas in a traditional family model both parties need to work and bring in two incomes.

This means that the childcare needs to be added into the mix increasing the need to make even more money. Grandparents are often now relied on more than prior years. Let's not forget that grandparents have worked their whole life with the dreams of retirement to now be babysitting to reduce costs on the family unit. This is causing fatigue for many grandparents. And of course many families do not have this option.

Relationships are not surviving, often due to stress and financial burdens—one true way to separate two previously loving people. So more and more solo parenting is happening. The systems support solo parents to some degree but does not take into account other challenges that often surround separation or divorce. Throw trauma in there, an increase in the effect on our mental illness, and it's diabolical.

# Wealth—The Allocation of Financial Support Is Not Equitable

What do you think immediately when you read this statement?

From a community perspective we see many issues and ones few have answers for. For those that know me they know that from my upbringing I have been involved in a lot of charity work. I have seen the poor effect on donors through fatigue and once successful projects close suddenly due to lack of funding. So I became an advocate for Social Enterprise, which are sustainable, commercially viable business models that serve social causes. Why? Because they are more long lasting and can be funded by investors who desire a return on investment, and why shouldn't they?

These enterprises can be self-funding through product sales, services, etc. and then do not need to beg, borrow, and manipulate people for funding. When the world fully grasps this model we will see change happen that brings ethical and well-thought-out services for our communities! Look into one charity serving a cause and you see 10 similar, all struggling to raise funds from the same generous people. Donor fatigue is rife, blocking numbers and becoming detached as they are being used. The contribution is imbalanced. Government could help this in so many ways but stay stuck in old ways.

*'There are new ways sitting right in front of us if we are prepared to disrupt our own mindset and re-educate ourselves. I see the solution so clearly but for the mainstream to get it will take years"*

Homelessness is on the rise, with a prediction of women over 50 being the segment of our community at risk. They cannot get work easily and if not trained in running a business, then the money stops. They can no longer afford housing and so end up in share houses. This is already happening. If you do not fit into a box you do not get support. If you have no savings, you will be a part of this epidemic. Families rarely look after their elders in the Australian culture and they end up in nursing homes or living alone.

Our system for crisis is rife. At only 43 years old I faced circumstances that I would never in a million years have imagined. I too became a statistic of domestic violence, financial abuse, fraud, and the list goes on. In crisis I thought I had no choice but to turn to Centrelink. I was still so embarrassed that someone like me could get trapped in such a bad way so few people in my life knew. I was given $200 to get me through. This was the beginning of a significant lack of support from the government I had paid taxes to. Just because my precious life had been wealthy should not mean I could not get help. I was directed to an amazing organisation, DV connect, and their services to this day have been extraordinary. I have subsequently sent nine women to their services and all are now safe from violent relationships. I was given access to Victim Assist and told to wait nine months for a response! Good luck finding support in the short term unless you have a child, as if a woman without children holds less importance.

Eighteen months later and nothing, not a call from a case manager or any form of support. I never expected handouts but I deserved help like any other woman.

They do not have enough funding and the filtering process appears poor. I referred other women there and they got immediate funds if children were involved. Why are children of greater importance than me? If I had children I would have been supported. A major flaw in our system.

To this day I was lucky to have incredible friends deposit funds into my bank and after months I was able to pay it all off with pride and launch myself into work. What I never had was support from the community to just stop and breathe and have full trauma support. This is part of my future mission, because things have got to change!

Did you know that if you have any form of mental illness written on your health record from a GP that this impacts income protection insurance? I of course have been suffering from PTSD and the rest of the symptoms that anyone who has experienced being beaten up would have. Miscarriages are also not considered trauma and yet I was rushed to hospital for complications twice, then required anaesthetic and time off work. Nothing covered.

So take care with insurance, because most humans have some form of challenge documented.

I am determined to see our community structures improve! They must!

## Health—The Collective Stress Is Causing Many Humans to End Their Lives

What do you think immediately when you read this statement?

I am sure we can all agree that there is a major rise in stress and stress-related illnesses. We are seeing autoimmune diseases become common and yet no treatment as such or cures exist for any of them. How can we heal inflammation when we are subjected to toxins in our skies with the weather engineering and chemtrails. With toxic foods, inaccurate food labelling, chemicals in our products, more pharmaceutical products, toxic water, etc.?

The mainstream model for wealth creation means working harder which equals more stress on our bodies. The need to make more money to match our lifestyle means more arguments around money resulting in divorces as one of the possible outcomes. Fatigue kicks in and then one's ability to keep up with work is diminished.

Separation of family units means more stress and solo parents are often in survival mode. Survival mode means less connecting within our communities and suffering in silence, just trying to keep our heads above water. A disconnected human presents to a local GP and antidepressants are prescribed, many causing suicidal tendencies. People are misdiagnosed for their sadness and then positioned into the shamed mental health category.

A powerful way to heal any stress is rest. But to rest one needs money or space to be able to. If you choose the natural route like I did it will cost you large sums of money. Money for natural medicines. Healing treatments such as acupuncture, acutonics, chiropractor, sound healings, breathwork, infusions, and so much more. So you need money to be able to rest and be healed. I have seen people go into healing crisis and never really come out, because they could not afford the supportive treatments they desperately needed. They are conscious enough to realise more drugs will not heal them. And continuing to work will end up in collapse. Know that one well!

Things are changing and so your real concerns can be overcome; in fact, they need to be overcome but may take a shift in perspective and survival strategies.

Amongst my peers we are saying often it takes a village to raise a child and yet we are not building villages. And even if we were there is such a major correction to the way we operate that would need to happen to create harmonious environments anyway.

I have seen the major human conflict in many eco villages that have been built. Belief systems for the environment did not necessarily match belief systems for how humans treat each other.

When I lived in Bali, I had a beautiful villa. I had a team around me to manage my health needs and the management of the home. I was the healthiest and energetic I have ever been, although I am well on my way there now. Through my recent reinvention period,

I again have created a team around me to manage so much so that rest could become the priority. I could not imagine life without this. I think we all deserve this level of support. It reduces stress indeed.

To this day, kindness and acceptance will help many conditions. Not being so alone and feeling loved and supported is one of the greatest human experiences. Self-healing is beyond comprehension. It is so powerful. Shaming of those not there yet is also harmful so take care in judgement in others.

The health of our communities will increase when we slow down, begin to love ourselves, and also include each other with all our unique needs and preferences.

There are many radical diets and lifestyle choices being presented for us to choose from. But one size doesn't fit all. We all have unique genetic make-ups and forcing a way of being on another is low vibration in its essence. I have felt shamed by vegan movements and judged at times. It hurt at the time but I now see it more than ever, the unresolved wounding some humans have is what hurts, not their choices. To shame those who have not converted is no different to shaming someone who does not join a particular religion.

So be conscious of your choices, use your discernment about what your body needs, and stay open to all choices. I am an advocate for animals. I have done every diet you can imagine, including fasting on water, so I am well educated and versed in health choices. I intuitively am guided to a low animal product diet in most instances and high plant based but I do not label myself anything. Because there are times we need different nutritional intakes based on healing needs of our incredible bodies which are healing machines.

We are often pulled apart through media channels and a fragmentation is being created within communities. It is always an eye-opener when I join new communities and hear of the separation and judgement. I would say I am living in one of the most stunning places on earth, filled with high vibrations, stunning nature, and incredible restaurants (ahhh, the food!), and yet some would judge this place.

What if we accepted that each part of our community focused on the improvement of one part? We could align in common activities without the rejection of others. Living in harmony. Okay, maybe I desire the perfect world, but I can choose to not sit in any camp. In fact I try and understand as many perspectives as I can. It balances me as a human being.

In a week where I live now, I can walk to the top of mountains and meditate at sunrise then go and eat breakfast from incredible chefs to then swim with whales, then write for hours. I can then do breathwork and meet my spiritual community. Then it's off to an art gallery and into a craft activity. Every possible human experience exists and all attract different types of people. I love not fitting into any of it and swimming in and out as I choose. True liberation!

We are in an US versus THEM war; it causes hatred and disconnection and it is not necessary! There is beauty in it all.

## Self—The Lone Wolf Has Left the Pack

What do you think immediately when you read this statement?

Another issue we see in society and one I know very well is the lone wolf syndrome (my words for it). It is not an easy chapter to move through and also becomes so stunning in its silence. In my experience when we experience high levels of stress, trauma, loss, or illness, the first thing we do is remove ourselves from the normal flow of life. We do this to regain energy, rest our systems, and survive in the first instance. The side effects of this are enormous and I experienced this in the 12 months after my last relationship ended.

When trauma happens we need to sometimes redefine our sense of safety within our community while we are healing. Often fragmentation happens and loss of relationships occur because people find the situation confronting or are seriously insensitive or simply are not in your life for the tough times. Distrust can occur on some level and so isolation becomes a part of the survival mechanism. But after that period what happens is what can cause many to never reintroduce themselves into the community.

The crashes are real! The world keeps going on and you are often left alone and really feeling isolated with few to connect to. I have especially seen it in people who lead others, teachers or influencers. Suddenly you have nothing left to give and you retreat to the quietest place possible. This process can go for months and even years for many. After removing yourself this can slowly affect income-flowing activities and of course the most important healing tool for all, love and connection.

I know the lone wolf stage well, it has come and gone through many of my major triggers to reinvent myself and it's been the hardest part of all.

So, if you know this place or are even in it, I relate to you and I feel you. If you are surrounded by people but still feel so alone inside, I get it. If you are super successful in your work but feel loneliness often in the middle of the night and even a sense of being misunderstood, I get it!

And our systems are not really designed to help us. Communities are trying but so often this lone wolf is hidden away so as to avoid embarrassment or be labelled a failure. The suffering is done in secrecy and causes many to end their lives. Some push through and crash with illness, some leave us, and some are struggling in silence.

The movement RUOK is a great start for one day of the year but what we need is to slow down, connect, and listen to each other every day. I call it slow down to speed up—the concept of slowing down so much that we witness stored traumas, release them, and then begin to investigate manifestation and the beauty of creation from a far more grounded and energised position.

We can do more for the community. One of my weekly practices now is to tune in and listen more, extend offers to invite people, those isolated, into my circle like a few dear friends of mine have done, and create as much inclusion as I can. I can do more now I am energised but a few special angels did this for me. And I am deeply grateful to them. They kept me in life. They kept me desiring to live even in the darkest days.

## The Good News!

*"The good news is we are seeing some emerging trends that support the reinvention of communities. More individuals are standing for strong connected communities!"*

1. More people are talking about affordable housing in anticipation of the need for people in our coming years. A conscious approach to a future homelessness problem locally.
2. Regenerative health centres are set up so we are starting to see a more holistic approach to health in general. The

next step is funding for this as Medicare has little part in supporting us become better human beings.

3. New communities are emerging outside the matrix to create a new way of connecting with strong integrity and new belief structures.

## Let's Look at This From a Personal Perspective—What Is Happening in Me?

*"Wealth equals security, so I will keep pushing to get more"*

It is true that we as humans need a sense of security, so we create security according to societal constructs. This security seeking causes us to make decisions to work more which causes emotional stress and spiritual disconnection. This stress then begins to break us down. We keep pushing more and more until life pushes us and we cannot go on.

What is working for us from a personal perspective? Are we striving for more? Are we driven by the need for more to demonstrate success or are we simply trying to survive in a world that feels like it is becoming harder and harder to keep up with?

## Wealth—Money Is the Solution to Happiness

What do you think immediately when you read this statement?

This often splits groups as many strive for more holidays and a nicer house. They dream of financial freedom and believe money will bring them everything they ever needed. The other group believe money is the root of all evil, rejecting it and therefore struggle throughout life rebelling about being part of it.

I know these both intimately; I have created a stunning flow of wealth and after losing my company embraced minimalism and a frugal perspective, pretending I loved it. I know lack and fear about money and I also know abundance and ease of creation. There are so many sides. But I much prefer abundance every time!

We are always hearing that wealth brings us happiness and in some ways I can agree. But it's the desperate need for it that is the problem more than the actual wealth.

Happiness comes from a far deeper belief system than external things. Comfort and luxury enhance our experience but are not the creator of happiness and never have been.

Often it's the getting out of struggle and stress that many dream of. The ability to make choices and not have to consider the financial implications.

We are fed that wealth is the answer to everything. Happiness and freedom all comes from having lots of money. So we are educated to get a job and we are taught that a job will bring us security. But although jobs can create a sense of security, you are in fact placing your future in someone else's hands. Companies come and go. You may also spend your life studying and get great jobs then hit 40+ and not be employable anymore and this is something I see often.

Employment can give you a sense of security for a period of time, it requires you to show up and a company is contracted to pay you. Our systems love to support those in jobs with home loans and financial access to opportunity. Having left the job world at age 30 I have watched my friends in jobs go through as much struggle as me in business land. So it's a choice, both have an up and down side.

So then people decide to leave a job to start a business. Often with no education or investment in training. Without education you can expect a higher chance of failure in business.

Anyone can start a business which puts people in massive danger of loss and ending up homeless or getting into government payouts or further debt.

Some of these people end up back in jobs or become unemployable due to burnout, loss of money, or unforeseen circumstances.

Modern day education companies share the next best thing but so often expect people to at least have a basic level of knowledge in which many employees transitioning do not have. I have trained in many business skills outside of nursing and pharmaceuticals and I have had many failures but also found my flow within it all. So for me to jump into a strategy is not so hard now, but for many they struggle to transfer their skills across.

The models that are available require confidence, investment, risk taking and for many it's too scary to begin these types of models. I encourage this because it can turn many lives around but you need to be ready and aligned to what you choose. Not every strategy works for every individual.

So the ever-flowing cycle of success, failure, energy in, money back, and everything in between is the cause of much exhaustion for so many. If you are reading this book I can guess however that you are seeking a new way and this is an area I am very passionate about!

I have experienced many models and seen great success both personally and with clients. It comes down to, do you want to be doing this daily practice of actions to succeed in this model? And does this model really align to my real passion or genius abilities?

If it's a no it is generally short lived; if it is a yes, like human transformation and social enterprise activities, for me it is a yes.

In the short term, we may engage in external consulting for a direct flow of money whilst we take up a new business model or strategy as it is often too much to take it on with zero resources. Especially if you are healing.

Shame or self-judgement is not valuable here, what you need is all that matters.

We ebb and flow with what our capacity is at each stage. I have always believed a movable multiple income stream model is a safe bet and I will share more about this in our online community.

## Health—Striving to Be Healthy Is Causing More Stress

What do you think immediately when you read this statement?

What does it mean to be healthy? How do we gauge if someone is healthy and what healthy is meant to look like?

The concept of being healthy is being influenced by so many factors. Who is the most powerful marketer of a product, a fad diet, or a promise of healing? The confusion about what works for who and how is bigger than ever and this industry is full of misinformation.

We see major sports being sponsored by alcohol companies, we see the image of a super low body weight supermodel as something to strive towards, and the new fasting protocols can create yo-yo dietary habits and energy crashes.

And I have been through them all!

The one thing they all create is a sense of expectation of being something we are not and then stress to try and get there with the concept that one size fits all.

The recent "keto craze" is a great example with so many jumping on the multiple products and recipes. And for many it is a highly effective option. But for many it is not. Keto and high fat made me feel very sick, my body couldn't convert the fat properly and I gained weight; I certainly never lost it! So I failed at yet another protocol that was supposed to work. Not a fun feeling when it promises to help every Tom, Dick, and Mary!

The concept of health is becoming confusing with people thinking diet and exercise is the whole health picture and god bless those who have the perfect genetic disposition to tolerate this as their plan.

But often stress comes through dieting and exercise for many and we feel forced to have our bodies match society's norms. We begin young and patterns of obsessions form. I know extremely anxious and stressed-out people who have the perfect-looking body. I see obsessive patterns of fasting and eating to look a certain way; I meet marathon runners who spent their lives running end up with autoimmune diseases, cardiac issues, and burnout.

Health is far deeper than this and there are so many more factors.

I have met health consultants who are stress heads with crappy relationships. Sorry, but this doesn't seem healthy to me. A self-obsessed gym bunny who adds in supplements to look better but has liver failure and lives with anxiety concerns me too.

Health is not working 50+ hour weeks and drinking all weekend to relax.

Burnout is on the rise and it is due to stress; the healthiest people who diet and exercise often end up completely shattered. Burnout is far more than physical. Emotional demands of families can turn a once fit person downhill fast. Chemical imbalances are occurring and the biochemistry for high achievers can become a nightmare. I know this one well. After an eight-week tour my biochemistry was off the scale and the comedown to more normal levels was debilitating. I had insane levels, it was incredible that I made it through. The outdated teachings that are supposed to develop a strong mindset with statements like "go hard or go home" are destructive to a depleted body. They are misguided and generalised. And yes, I took it all on and it made me sick.

I am seeing my fellow women falling like flies, collapsing in stress, anxiety higher than ever, and suicidal thoughts increasing. So many want to give up through sheer exhaustion and depletion of their systems.

Many women are choosing not to have children due to economic costs and also the struggle of managing both families and careers. Infertility is high in the healthiest women for no reason.

Radical movements such as the vegan movement are taking hold with guilt and shaming everywhere for those not ready to convert to a high soy-based and plant-based diet which is not necessarily healthy for all body types. And of course vegans are being shamed for their choices too. It's all out of whack!

From every angle in general to those I have interviewed many are feeling despondent and sick of the constant pressures of trying to keep up.

# Self—Being Responsible for Everything in Your Life Is Causing High Stress

What do you think immediately when you read this statement?

Just because one guru stood on stage and said we are responsible for everything doesn't mean we are responsible for everything. I cannot control the weather or the chemtrails. I do not control my genetic disposition although I can self-heal. I cannot take responsibility for your crappy behaviour and we should not be responsible for an entire race of humans who are being controlled by systems outside our control.

There, you have it ! My view!

Look, I get the personal development industry and their attempts at making us a more accountable race. And I have become a great woman because of some of the teachings. But the generalised projection of concepts only causes a greater sense of failure, depression, and unrealistic expectations. And that does not serve us.

I have been told in my past that I was often extreme in my views, and I would agree now, looking back. But being extreme or highly committed to my goal was celebrated in the personal development world I lived in. On my recent tours I was told by other speakers on countless occasions of how insane I was to tour that many events. But in that industry what I did was expected or even the norm. So it's all perspective.

Having had an enormous shift, nowadays I celebrate how many days I have focused on the work I love, like writing, creating retreats, and sharing stories. I celebrate how deep my rest is. I celebrate my type of movement and what it gave me. I celebrate how many times

I slow down to speed up and make up my own mind about life. It is a different formula for success and a much more sustainable one.

Being over-responsible is a major issue amongst many of the successful people I have met.

When it comes to health, and through my most recent energetically depleted stage, I entered the medical system through an emergency situation (not my choice!). A diagnosis would bring clarity to those I worked with and those who needed a framework to understand my depletion. My friends who knew me well just wanted me to trust in self-healing which has been the most effective paradigm of all. But I entered the system in case I needed it later on. I surrendered into the situation but noticed I blamed myself for being unwell.

A dear friend said to me, "You are one of the most committed people to health I know." I appreciated that and realised I was not giving myself any credit. It must have been my choice of food or lifestyle, it had to be. But it was not. As you read in my story so much more was happening in my life than diet.

Trauma affects everything. A genetic disposition plays a significant role. Life situations can make us unwell. And pressure to be perfect is a definite one!

I can't be responsible for the genetic disposition my father passed to me and he is now dead. If he was alive I could have it out with him but he died when I was 15 years old!

And I also believe that much is created through our thoughts, decisions, and actions, but not everything. Too often comments are thrown around when someone is in the depths of pain that lack enormous empathy and compassion. You need kindness at this stage, nothing else. Love, connection, and empathy. Our society has a long way to go with this, especially with mental illness and autoimmune diseases. Cancer seems to be more understood, thanks to awareness campaigns, and the judgement far less. All humans deserve kindness when they hit a major upgrade symptom!

A leader I work with was presenting the other day on a webinar and he said, "You know, we create everything, even cancer." On the call was a friend of mine who had recently come through cancer. Crazy! Please, I hope we can stop this type of random commenting without real connection to what we are saying. And yes, the friend knew that his stress needed to be released but he also had a major genetic disposition to cancer. He was also of perfect body weight and followed all the regimes. He is a high achiever and yes, he does drink alkaline water. But he got cancer. There is far more than we know so often. Acceptance is the first step and then supported healing, and ultimately self-healing.

As humans I believe we need to take care in throwing around perspectives without embodying empathy for others. It's different if your partner got cancer tomorrow. I doubt you would say to them, "See, you created that!"

Our insensitivity and over responsibility is cruel and unkind; yes, it's used to wake people up but if that is your strategy to wake people up I think most leaders would challenge your own personal world.

# The Good News!

*"The good news is we are seeing some emerging trends that support the reinvention of us as a human race. Empathy is building. Awakening is happening at a rapid rate. Higher levels of support are coming forth and kindness, love, and connection are being recognised as the foundations of being human"*

1. More people are sourcing the aligned wealth vehicles that allows for integration of lifestyle needs and happiness. They are open to new online businesses that can support balance.
2. People are starting to command that their wellness comes first and reframing what health looks like. New treatments are emerging, and stress and anxiety is being recognised more publicly.
3. People are challenging old paradigms and starting to turn inwards and using discernment in their choices. Kindness is emerging. Empathy is being asked for. Compassion is growing.

# CHAPTER 5

# THE WHOLE SELF PHILOSOPHY

In the last chapter, we opened to some perspectives from a global, community, and personal perspective for the purpose of opening up our minds and beginning to consider the concept of questioning our chosen reality. I encouraged you to make your own minds up. I do not see anything as black and white, I never have. Grey, red, yellow, and blue are colours too! So allow yourself to play with your own perspectives.

To reinvent we need to be able to unpack, disrupt old paradigms. and consider the upgrade stages next. Before we go into the human reinvention formula, let's look at the concept of a "whole self."

One of the concepts that many old models talk about is balance. The ever-driving motivation to feel balanced or have a balanced life, but I do not see many humans who get or have really experienced balance. I guess it all comes down to what balance means to you.

Exhausting and intense weeks or months of busyness then a holiday to return and do it all again is not a model that suits all. Also a model I used to do was "working holidays," so coupling work and play together. Then realising that I had never really had a real holiday in years. I had to relearn how to relax fully.

So how do we create a whole self philosophy, a way of being that allows for a fulfilment of so many more parts of ourselves amongst paradigms and systems that dictate certain ways of operating? I do not believe it is a one-size-fits-all approach but a process of recognising within ourselves what we really need. Not what social norms are because we do not all fit into that interpretation.

When we look at the way we operate and focus in life, we can consider the make-up as five parts of a whole. Of course there are many more parts or sub-groups but for the purpose of finding your own reality around this we will focus on five. All parts have their relevance so we have an option to consciously define how we flow with each part at each stage of life in what way. To deliberately choose this is to be the superhero in our own story.

The belief "we can have it all" can be absolutely true. I have always felt drawn to this concept but what I never considered in my younger years was when each part had its significance according to my own internal meter, when it would be expressed, so I just tried to do it all!

My life never seemed to match society's time frames for anything so I had to make my own path up. I didn't grow up with the normal dreams of having a job, owning my own home, getting married, and having two children. It wasn't until much later in life that I even saw value in this and it was still in a rather less conventional way. Not sticking to the norm meant being misunderstood and having to work around a system that saw life as one way. (This is changing but ever so slowly.)

I have learnt that age does not need to determine anything except perhaps fertility but even that is debatable. I meet so many people living by numbers; in my view to do that is to feel very lost when you hit 60. I will be around a long time so what happens to the last 30+ years. No way am I taking on that mainstream approach!

So although society may say one thing, I choose to walk to the beat of my own drum. I encourage you too!

You might find following the societal norms does not gel like a perfect calendar of events for you, but perhaps have not challenged them before. You may find you did follow the path of getting married when your friends did to be one of the ones who also divorced many years later. That is almost a norm now too. Then you do solo parenting as many others do. I have heard friends even say they feel cheated. They followed the plan and it did not work out for them.

So we get to make up our own version and our own timing. You can take the pressure off and ride your own set of waves!

The five parts we will look at and apply the formula to are Wealth, Self, Energy, Community, and Contribution.

## Let's Define Wealth—Your Wealth-Building Vehicles

Wealth can be defined in many ways. Your whole wealth picture is far more than money flow and income. Wealth can be expressed as richness in life, relationships, and energy, but for the purpose of this book we separate wealth out into a topic around income-producing activities or investments. These are the ways in which you choose to bring in income. Your work or career. Your business or your investments. Residual income from properties or shares.

There are so many ways to build your wealth and so often we fall into a pathway that does not in fact align to what we really need. Multiple income streams has always been my preference and has served me well over the years.

Here are some of the ways people bring in income:

- Employee—You work for someone else
- Self-employed—You work as a consultant for a business
- Direct selling, network marketing—You sell products within networks
- Business owner—You build your own system online or offline
- Investing—You leverage your money to make more money

Our mainstream education system in general teaches us the basics to make directional decisions about our future at a young age. There has been much criticism that we are teaching our next generation old ways, therefore new, alternative education facilities are emerging.

When I lived in Bali I visited the Green School and was in awe of the environment. The whole school was built out of the most magnificent bamboo structures. The teachings were experimental and I imagined myself learning in that way. So impressive. I guess in many ways I did learn that way as a lot of my education was travelling to different countries with my mum, setting up toy libraries and social projects.

So as a child you reach a point of needing to decide what path you will take, often influenced by parents. For me it was nursing or drama school. I chose nursing because it meant I could travel and that was what fired up my belly.

You then walk your education path and get a job.

But for the percentage of children who are naturally entrepreneurial spirits they will often get crushed in a traditional system. Some of us find our way eventually but again it involves large amounts of money to be able to re-educate ourselves later in life.

Gosh, being different is an expensive luxury, it seems, isn't it?

So most of us begin as employees; many stay that way but dream of the next stage daily as they commute back and forth to a job with little free time for anything else.

For some the drive to become self-employed comes early and they go on a journey into a land with often little education. In the excitement of leaving their boss they embrace the journey of owning their own hours. Some end up doing even more work than before but celebrate the freedom. I have seen friends lose so much freedom they become burnt out and unhappy until mastery comes, of course. Being self-employed has always been my default as I transition. It means I can consult, coach, or mentor with little extra business creation to do and results in immediate cash flow.

Another option is the home-based business of which there are many types of models. Some are taking on a small business working with a big company, like a direct selling company or networking style. You in essence become a brand ambassador for their products, but you gain the freedom of working in your own home with your own time frames. Many love this option as it can bring in a residual income which is sales commissions online through customer usage of the products. Home-based businesses used to hold a real stigma but we are seeing these types of businesses become more common. But do not be fooled: they still require some skills with people and products. I have had great success with this model at certain stages of my life.

Next stage is becoming a business owner, and this is one to be considered. General schooling may not prepare you for what this takes. Why they do not educate on starting businesses in schools is beyond me. Would save a lot of wastage of time and money down the track, not to mention heartache!

When I built my first business, I attracted in investors and mentors to build with. This was a blessing and a curse. But it accelerated the growth and we reached incredible heights in such a space of time. I was new and fresh when I built that business. I loved the ride of building. I loved the impact we made and I loved the revenue we produced! I loved having such an incredible team! They say many businesses fail. I say all businesses bring enormous growth and big waves. But for me it is the most fulfilling ride of a lifetime.

Your own business can be offline brick and mortar or online. The online world of creating your own products, programmes, and services is extensive but I highly recommend you begin with a mentor. I have begun online education businesses and selling products online like Amazon. You can build with Airbnb, healing retreats, pretty much anything...

I love the freedom of creating online businesses. And from experience I highly recommend you get educated. Then your chances of success are much higher.

And then there are investments. Property is a common one as it can bring such high returns. I love property for the fruit it bears! Shareholding and selling or trading are a preference and I have loved the success for me in shares. Many are afraid of shares; I say, just choose your mentors wisely. Trust your intuition on whom you learn from. A business colleague of mine is incredible, so ethical and grounded. Bitcoin or cryptocurrencies have been volatile but also produced great income for some. I see flaws in that system too but never close off to its potential.

There are so many options for you! If your wealth world needs reinvention then open your mind. I am passionate about seeing people work the right vehicle for them. I get frustrated when experts pretend every strategy will work for every person, it is not true. But taking the time to select your vehicle is critical. Do your due diligence and don't get hyped up in false claims, for which there are many. Feel free to tap into our community and we can guide you on this. I do affiliate to some education but only if I have done it myself or been involved in it. I am happy to share my view. At the end of the day it's your choice which way to go.

Beginning a new business with no money is never recommended; work a little longer and save funds. The lack of mindset that is present when you have no money can cause two reactions: a-fight-for-what-you-need approach or in many cases "I cannot see the future clearly." Work with someone with an abundant mindset to elevate your mindset first then choose your strategy and be all in.

Always enter a new opportunity with an "all in" approach. A fence-sitting, will-this-work approach will never serve you!

Building wealth is one of my favourite parts of myself; I love to create, I love to be focused, and I love the variety. But it needs to be in sync with my other needs or burnout occurs.

## Let's Define Self—Your Self-Expansion

Self-expansion is the way you work on your growth as a human being. It is the conscious part of your life or it can also happen through simply living life fully. Either way is fine but I am guessing if you choose to read this book, you are looking to be very aware on how you can move through life as your whole self in a new way.

How you choose to expand as a human being and find greater levels of fulfilment is of your own choosing and we are all attracted to different ways. In my experience there is not one way through this life. But the one thing about self is it is uniquely yours. So you need to make yourself important enough to be alone and still to grow. If we live in co-dependent relationships or make our family number one we might miss the opportunity for self to be so very important.

I see so many mums give up everything they need for their children, thinking that is what is required. It's dangerous and builds resentment, breaks up families, and can create a loss of identity. They are not to be blamed as often time is already so stretched but to show your children a pathway into becoming an adult would be valuable and can be done in being one yourself. I asked my mum how she managed this with us four children, one with special needs and both working parents and travelling. She said that in today's world she sees parents trying to be so perfect and control so much. Get it right all the time. Overdo activities, to the point of exhaustion. In her day, she lived her life fully by working and travelling and we came along for the ride. This worked for her and us, but each family is of course individual.

The choices you make around your importance of self can lead you down many different paths. This is the richness of your unique expression. Your spiritual insights or worldly views of life. How you bring in daily joy and contentment. How you feel happy and love.

Some ways to build self-expansion are:

- Developing a strong presence through self-evaluation
- Joyful practices
- Expanding your community
- Experiencing new adventures
- Spiritual growth

I have always been a deep thinker. I have observed humans since I can remember, so self-evaluation became a normal part of life, hence it is a strength. But at times it became over expressed. My critical mind took over and began to undo me at times. To just be in a day can bring as much joy and expansion then thinking about it. The hyper vigilant mind is one to be aware of for this can sabotage us rather rapidly.

Self-evaluation is not about blaming ourselves or picking the faults in our character. It is a simple process of checking in. How do I feel? And how do I feel under that layer? And under the next? It's a truthful account of my experience of myself. This can become a daily ritual as we slow down and become more present.

Presence is still one of the greatest gifts we have. It can be hard work to be present for busy, high-paced people. Slowing down the mind and body to listen can feel impossible. If we are storing emotions we will often avoid slowing down in fear of collapsing and not being able to get back up. I know this one well. Distraction has become a form of coping for many.

What about the choosing of activities or practices that bring you joy? I had forgotten about this at many stages of my reinvention. Joy seemed so far away and hard to access. Everyone would say, do gratitude practices, they are so powerful, but I could not feel gratitude in some of these moments. And that was scary. So we need to begin on a very simple level. I found remembering when I had last felt joy was one of my ways to begin to envision joy as a close friend again. Just be happy, they say, have fun, socialise with those you love! It's the last thing one can access when you are depleted.

As I have moved through the tough times I found joy in whole new ways that gave me so much energy. My friend and I laugh about me being a crazy cat lady and it is a label for someone who is so passionate about animals, particularly the felines. I would lie on the lounge so depleted and exhausted and just watch them play. Simple joy from simple things. I would drag myself out of bed each morning for sunrises, just to see something of beauty. It helped me reset each day. Sun gazing at sunrise is still one of my most impactful practices to this day. Then when I moved to Noosa it was whale watching on the deck. Ahhh!

I still squeal with joy when I see those majestic creatures launch out of the ocean gracefully!

Expanding my reach into community took a little longer but once I entered new spaces it gave me big doses of energy and insight. I joined community acupuncture sessions and meditations, gentle gatherings where I could be as quiet as I needed to be. Sitting in a local café, just being around others. Searching for new groups and activities I had not previously considered. Playing with new crafts or opportunities to be present became a weekly activity. Today

I now do so many things I never expected and have met more incredible human beings who are continuing to show me new ways of being human!

The next stage of self was the creation of a new bucket list. I had given up on this years back as I had travelled so much, ticked so many things off the list, and done so many adventures. My life had been one big bucket list. But it was time to bring it back in a new way.

So I sat and read magazines and dreamed of new adventures with new people. Things I had not done or things I wanted to repeat. Observe how you may block possibilities if you link them to wealth. That is when my passion for whales came to light. Suddenly invites to go to Tonga came to light and if my energy had been higher I would have gone. 2020 watch out!

I decided to reinvent my passion for food. I had lived in a bubble of fear around reactions to food as I swelled up with so much in my past but it was time to break through that. With a new friend we began a list of top restaurants and we started ticking them off!

I decided to join music groups and began saying yes to things I would not have said yes to previously. And life began to expand!

And spiritual growth came easily. I was lucky to have chosen to move to an area that was full of interesting opportunities to engage in soul-expanding and soul-centred activities. I booked in new activities, found my place in some, and would never return to others. It became a challenge to do something new each week. I could see my soul starting to smile again!

Self is so very important, but it need not be a chore. Playing with newness with self becomes fun. Getting started is the key.

# Let's Define Energy—Your Energy Force

Your life force, the energy that moves through your body beyond only the physical. The ways in which your energy is generated in your life and how it translates out into your wealth-building activities and all aspects of being human. This is far more than exercise and nutrition. The piece that is often unobserved is understanding what activities feed your energy and what depletes you. And also understanding the biochemistry of stress so you can create a model that ensures your physical and energetic body is able to manage life's requirements.

Some ways to build your energy force are:

- Deep rest practices—meditation, silence
- Nature-filling activities
- Fasting or resting of the physical system
- Specialised nutrition practices plus heal gut your emotional centre
- Infrared saunas, float tanks, acutonics, acupuncture, ice baths, breathwork
- Biohacking

When life is crashing or you feel depleted or under stress, slowing down into silence and meditation can be a far too extreme goal to achieve, the gap too big and mission too extreme. They say rest and I say how! When your pace is fast or your brain's processing is manic then it can feel daunting to slow down. I hear of the fear some people feel about the collapse if they were to slow down. And so often holidays become a chance for the body to crash to rest often  resulting in illness. So we need to avoid this cycle as it does not serve us.

To begin to build silence in your life is magic; you can add in a simple 10 minutes a day away from people, technology, and stimulation. Then do this for three days and increase it to an hour a day. Then two hours if you can.

Active meditation can be easier to embrace on a lunch break or when out walking; you can listen and do these at the same time. It allows you to move at your own pace and yet still allow your mind to focus into a peaceful state. Meditation does not need to look like the monk on the hill, sitting in silence. And this is often a too big jump for many.

Nature is a fast one for slowing your system; a gentle walk in nature can do wonders for our systems. Or heading to the beach which can be a more stimulating energy but a nice step towards slowing until you are ready for the quiet of the forest or mountains. The key is to get out of reach of technology like modems, phones, and computers. This will be a wonderous gift. Turning off modems for certain times of days. Having curfews on usage is useful too. And watch your system settle. For me this is always a profound shift.

If you live in a busy city, find your local park or beach and get out every single day without fail.

Fasting has been a big part of my life and an energy boost in most cases. Beginning with a gentle intermittent fast then on to whole days on juice and even water fasting once you have prepared your system. Water fasting takes you to new places beyond your body, here I have created my most powerful projects. But you need to listen to your system. In my recent reinvention fasting came after three months of settling the system as it would have been dangerous to do this sooner. So listen to your own needs, ask yourself, "Do I need to rest my digestive system right now?" You decide, no one else. This is not a fad, this is a way of life. But take care as I see people go too extreme too soon and end up in bed for days.I am guilty of that. No ego in fasting, There are gentle approaches and if you are reinventing right now, you need gentle to begin with.

Understanding energy and how it works goes beyond dieting but also into understanding your gut health and what is brewing there. So many emotional challenges are stored in our gut, past memories and fears too. There are many ways to heal the gut so go on the journey and find what feels in alignment to you. I have always been aware of gut health. But this round I was shocked to hear I had parasites in high doses that was affecting my ability to produce serotonin, resulting in a really flat mood. We fixed this and it gave me a whole lease on life. So listen to your body, get a bioscreen test if you like facts, and treat gently and in your own time. Most GP's do not suggest this or even consider gut health but you can research this online yourself.

You can add in a number of external energy supporting actions like magnesium baths daily then on to magnesium pool soaking and gentle conscious body movement. Infrared saunas to detox and learn to relax the system. High dose magnesium and other relaxants (all natural) to bring the system into a neutral state again. This took three months and is still something I am diligent with today.

Acupuncture can be a strong support treatment to align your energetic system. In my experience seeing someone who goes beyond the physical system and is trained in isoteric acupuncture or transformational acupuncture is worth experiencing. This allowed my system to go to new places. Acutonics is my all time favourite, I was blessed to work with an incredible woman based in Currumbin, Queensland, Australia and her work is off the scale powerful, I wish I could teleport her to Noosa to treat me weekly! And not to forget breathwork and ice baths.

Breathwork or rebirthing I began back in Bali over 8 years ago and this shifts you at your core. I have experienced profound expansion through breathwork and then went on to use this in ice baths. The 'Wim Hoff' method which we use to then sit in ice baths, I learnt many years back and it has served me for revitalisation but only when my physical system was stablished. A healing crisis can come too quickly if you attempt this on a depleted system.

And the part that opened my mind up most was "biohacking." Biohacking can be described as do-it-yourself biology. For me I was supported by my holistic GP in a regenerative clinic. For many "biohackers," this consists of making small, incremental diet or lifestyle changes to make small, yet powerful improvements in your health and well-being.

Looking at the biochemistry of the body gives you great data to work with. Within a week of identifying the imbalances we could treat this naturally and begin to produce a relaxing environment reducing anxiety and yoyo emotions almost immediately. Biohacking takes time to find your own sweet formula. It can bring heightened energy and deep grounding too.

As we biohack we may also consider removing toxins or distracting substances from our diet. You create your own path here. For some it may be reducing alcohol or any addictions. For others, types of food. Some activities that create too much stimulation at times when you need a rest. It's your life, you get to empower yourself. Guilt, blame, or self-loathing play no part! Do this with kindness. And in your own timing.

Energy is the force of life and there are so many ways to manage this. I wish for you that if your energy centre is struggling that you may open to a holistic approach beyond mainstream medicine and play with new ways to bring relaxation into the core of your cells. We all deserve to feel good and have energy that fuels our lives.

# Let's Define Community—Your Connection To Others

Community is who is around us and the ways in which we receive support from family, friends, and partners. The community we surround ourselves with, such as through our work or business, education, wellness and spiritual activities. Are they powerful connections that create energy or a sense of inclusion?

Some ways we connect to community:

- Regular time with those we love fully present
- Colleagues and peers
- Spiritual connections
- Education peers
- Connections through children's education

In my experience, community changes constantly, or more so, relationships change constantly. Ever evolving and expanding. I know this is probably not the norm and many people stay in the same place for much of their life. And this can halt growth in a big way. As I reinvent myself my needs literally shift and therefore so do my relationships. I love it this way. I of course have my long-term friends who will always be in my life as long as they have accepted my life changes and me theirs. It's about being able to connect at new levels. If not, the friendship fades away, hopefully always with love, although some struggle with this.

I used to feel bad about this but now I love myself more and I see that I get to choose how I am treated and who I give love to without obligation.

I seek more present relationships these days, ones that are high quality when we interact, and holding this intention has brought so many beautiful connections into my life.

You can actively choose. If it is not working can it grow and can you hold a light for it to? Or do you need to let it go? (always with love if possible)

Colleagues and peers also often change through the years as your beliefs shift and new business opportunities emerge. I love that about business: there are always new people to meet and delve into new projects with.

I have never been a great structured networker, I found those environments really unnatural for me. Where we sit around the table and hand out business cards. I always want to meet the real business behind the business but I still make myself go to some events.

Rather than networking, I prefer to hold intentions to connect. I am conscious about who I would like to meet and for what purpose, especially if looking to collaborate on a certain project. I do not stay in one group and constantly move also to expand out my community. I have many tribes for to have one feels limiting to me. Different tribes fulfil different needs. I love travel for connecting as I meet the most unlikely people.

My community also consists of those with a belief in a higher god or spirit. I love to meet in this space and rather than follow a dogma, I love to share, create, and experience new ways. I have always been curious about different religions; I like to stay open to others' choices. I find this keeps me honest.

Community might be through your children's activities or education. Community is everywhere and you can join as many as you choose.

Community needs to hold a sense of freedom for me, an open and flexible approach. That way I am never playing as an obligation rather a choice to bring my gifts to it voluntarily.

# Let's Define Contribution—Your Giving and Receiving

Contribution can hold many meanings for you. In your daily life you may feel you are contributing enough. If you find you are not giving out at all, it may mean you are depleted as you have nothing to give or you may have challenges trusting others. Whatever it is I encourage you to define this as it may just be blocking potential energy flow into your life.

Contribution has been a natural part of my upbringing. It was my parents' life to give back to the community and so I have seen many versions of contribution. But it is always your choice and should be giving you energy, not draining you of it.

I see many volunteers who give and give to the detriment of their own health. They never make money or give back to themselves, they become in service and we as a society celebrate those who have sacrificed their lives for good. They struggle in silence and then life becomes really difficult and often families need to then support them. They miss the opportunity to embrace their own wealth and self-worth.

This makes me concerned that this is the mentality of our society. We think it is okay to use humans with big hearts, without any return of income or support. I do not think this is functional on any level.

Many of these big hearted humans have no money, live off the smell of an oily rag and choose this. But I know many of these humans, and they dream of freedom and having their needs met.

To reinforce this behaviour is to reinforce martyrdom and a lack of self-love. They deserve a more whole self approach and it is their choice.

So giving out is wonderful, but learn to receive too.

You may either be giving and not receiving fully right now. Or not giving at this stage. Both lack the energy pulsing through you that one can experience when this is activated.

And I can talk from my life experience from both perspectives.

Contribution needs to match your capacity. For me, my most abundant years were when my business was flowing and I was giving to a project in need. Sometimes financially but often I would give my genius or my energy first. That way the cycle was still in flow at different stages of my own wealth journey.

Are you aware of sustainable ways of giving instead of old paradigms of endless donating?

I am a major advocate for social enterprise and the investing in projects that are sustainable. We need to ensure that there is also a strong ability to be able to receive as well. Not being able to receive is a major cause of burnout so therefore all contribution focuses need to be evaluated to ensure there is an exchange of giving and receiving. This is a process that can elevate you rapidly in the area of wealth. When you know how to fully receive on all levels.

Some ways to contribute are:

- Invest money in a sustainable model that serves a social purpose
- Support local community projects
- Receive help from the local community for what you need
- Receive help from friends or family
- Work on attracting support on all levels, financially and energetically

If you have excess income to invest then I encourage you to look at projects that have a sustainable future. What this means is, let's say you have $10k in a year to give to a cause.

You give $10k to a charity for the rescue of trafficked children, for example, and that feeds a number of children. It makes you feel good and you helped. That money runs out and the charity needs another $10k to rescue even more children.

But what if you gave $10k towards the building of a cafe that taught rescued children to then learn barista or hospitality skills? They then obtained training, jobs, and a new future. That $10k then began to produce profits and is reinvested into the cafe ongoing to create a self-sustaining business?

Which one would last longer?

Charities always need more donations, but social enterprises provide income to sustain themselves. Many charities who understand this are adding social enterprise projects alongside their charity work to allow for more reliable funds. Internationally we are seeing more of this, but Australia is still trying to grasp this concept. Even after speaking out on stages about this, the norm of most corporates is to donate to charity, No judgement of course but I really do wish they would use their commercial mindset when considering how money flows to support social causes.

Most humans do what we have always done until they know that there are more options. You can choose to contribute your money in a long-term, visionary way, supporting social enterprises become self-sufficient. This creates long term change!

MIAKO, the social enterprise I founded, has developed online education which can be sold over and over again to profit the enterprise. We then produce great ethical products that are sustainable and sell them for profit, reinvesting back into the business but also supporting other services globally to enhance their capacity to survive in business. A multifaceted approach.

If funds are not in excess for you then you can look at contributing resources, energy, or connections.

When I was touring I made a pact to speak about the trafficked children situation in every presentation. Today I still honor that commitment. That has no doubt led many people to organisations that support children getting out of sex slavery.

Your voice goes a long way with social issues, be loud and proud but be careful not to polarise anyone.

You can give time to causes and travel to a place that needs a school built or education. I travelled often to Thailand to help out where I could.

You could network people towards a cause or even tell people about this book which then funds MIAKO. 100% of profits from this book go directly into the MIAKO Fund to enable us to grow ongoing. MIAKO requires ongoing income flow to be able to educate more charities to embrace social enterprise. We also want to see more and more individuals who feel passionate about social change begin Social Enterprises so they may too become sustainable. MIAKO has the education to support these people.

So choose what will bring you energy and respect; if you are depleted then maybe it's not the time. But make a point to ensure the time comes to engage in contribution because the joy to be able to give back is magnificent and deeply energising.

My happiest moments in life have been being able to give back. But I have also needed to learn how to receive to balance this up.

Blocking your ability to receive can mean a great loss of energy, a sense of never realising your wealth potential fully, and a real sense of being alone.

Receiving is now something I value highly but it was not always this way.

People would say to me you need to learn how to receive but if it was just a mind decision it would be easy to do. I thought I was receiving. Until I began digging deeper and realised my default program was over-giving in most areas of my life.

Blocking one's ability to receive is deep and complex for most. And it goes back to a whole set of beliefs about ourselves and influences for society.

If you do not have a high sense of self-worth you may not believe you deserve wealth. Some people have always done it hard or watched their parents struggle so they think that is the norm.

Receiving can be financially, emotionally, or physically hard for some until the program is released and then it is delicious and wonderful!

This recent chapter has caused me to have to receive more than usual and it feels so lovely to receive human support after I had created a past community around me of solo survivors who all do most alone.

Do you have gaps in your giving and receiving and is there room to add this into your reinvention?

I hope you are able to experience this fully for the joys of giving are large and the love one receives through receiving is magical!

## Your Score

So, now let's review each of these five parts of your whole self and see where you are at. If you were to score yourself with each part now and add a number to it how would each part show up? Not in comparison to any other part, but standing on its own right now?

YOUR SCORE:

We measure this from a 1 to a 5. 1 is 'Not functioning well' and 5 is 'Exceptional and in flow'.

Review each area now.

- o WEALTH—Your wealth building
- o SELF—Your self-expansion
- o ENERGY—Your energy force
- o COMMUNITY—Your connection to others
- o CONTRIBUTION—Your giving and receiving

Choose your numbers and take time to really be honest with yourself. There is always room to shift this later when you use the formula! What did you notice?

As we move through different stages of life the levels that we operate at within each part change. And this is normal to witness. Some high achievers expect all parts to flow at all times, ha! I know that one. You may wonder why wealth may drop when you build your family. Or energy crashes after launching a new startup. Everything has its divine timing and flow, it is us that can get in the way!

Here are three examples over different stages so you can begin to understand this scoring:

In 2011, here were my scores:

- WEALTH (4)
- SELF (3)
- ENERGY (2)
- COMMUNITY(2) and
- CONTRIBUTION (4).

In 2015, here were my scores:

- WEALTH (3)
- SELF (4)
- ENERGY (2)
- COMMUNITY (2) and
- CONTRIBUTION (3).

In 2019, here were my scores:

- WEALTH (4)
- SELF (4)
- ENERGY (3)
- COMMUNITY(3) and
- CONTRIBUTION (2).

We can start to see patterns, so look at your patterns over the last seven years. My scores show some distinctive patterns. Wealth and Self have been a priority alongside Contribution, it has driven me. But even though I may have been healthy with a great diet, I struggled with the physical needs of my choices in career. The stressors of building businesses. Energy and Community have been areas that have not featured as high as others.

My own energy was down therefore I had less energy to integrate into other people's world. A cycle that continued until 2019 when I was able to begin reinventing this in a big way.

Make sure you do this for yourself and see what patterns emerge for you. We do this more extensively inside the online community. This is just the beginning, keeping it simple for you to begin opening to your whole self.

As we move through stages, each stage requires different levels of focus and energy and rarely is it ever in balance. So to strive for perfection in all areas is unrealistic for most. So it then comes down to choices and timing. The striving to have it all can become a big trigger for collapse. We can have it all but perhaps only when we remove stages of life and time frames. Then we can have it all!

But we rarely experience it all as we think it should be ... Life is far more mysterious than that!

# CHAPTER 6

# THE HUMAN REINVENTION FORMULA

What is the truth of your life right now?

We have set the scene with looking at what is outside of us which may affect our internal systems and also your whole self. I hope you have taken the opportunity to consider your beliefs about the world we live in and felt empowered to see how many options there are for you. Removing those constructs that do not support the life you need most is liberating.

So who are you and I wonder why you're reading this book of all books? What called you to consider reinvention? We so often hear people talk about their story. We all have one. Where we came from and how it has been for us all. Some paradigms say leave your story in the past and yet the most relatable part about humans is the sharing of stories. I say own your story and turn it into the most magnificent opportunity. Some of our stories are crappy and painful but to heal is to be able to move past the pain and trauma and own it.

This is different to avoiding your story, pretending it is not relevant or blocking it and acting as if it is all fine. A person I knew in my past used to say 'I walk through the fire and I don't come out smelling as smoke'. I used to think this was kind of powerful to say. Until I experienced a relationship challenge with this person and saw how they jumped from relationship to relationship leaving others in trauma with zero empathy and ignoring the destruction to others. Only to repeat the same pattern over and over with the next people they met. I prefer to say " I have been through the fire, I have been burnt, I have released deep insights and I have healed deeply to emerge a better human on all levels.'

This is my story, moving through and upgrading from the craziness of life. Imagine if all humans did this! Do not disempower your human experiences as they played an important role, be proud of what it has gifted you! And if you cannot see that yet be patient that is completely normal, then this book is perfect for you!

To own your story of your life and see how it influenced you is important. Our stories have influenced how we feel today. And they deserve acknowledging. I see so many teachers instruct humans to reject their story and move through them too quickly but all that does is create stored trauma. Which will arise later in life. Trust me, I tried that!

So OWN your story, the good, the bad, and the ugly! It's yours to play out.

Trauma, challenges, loss, heartbreak, and all the shitty parts of life are normal parts of life. A perfect life does not exist ...Hollywood movies have influenced my view for many years but there are not always happy endings in the way we have been shown. We all have had our own level of challenge and it is all significant. We have all been victims at some stage and also participated in far-from-perfect situations. We are humans—both dark and light! That is what makes us divinely human!

## Embrace Your Victim

Everyone who has ever done any personal development would have heard about "victim mentality." The "negative" mindset that says' "this happened to me and it's painful" and "someone else did this to me." It often comes with a lot of emotions and the person sometimes seems stuck in it, like they can't move on.

*Spoiler: The reality is that they can't because they aren't fully integrated yet so lay off them! Stop the judgement. They are human like you!*

The predominant teaching says this mentality is bad, that it won't get you anywhere you truly want to go and while I can agree to parts of the thinking behind this, it isn't considered a very important aspect in true self-healing and I believe it is very important.

We are human.

We experience, we think, and we feel. We love and we hurt. We are constantly in motion, always growing and evolving, and many of our experiences are not benign. Some are highly exhilarating, some are completely devastating and there's everything in between. It's all part of the human experience and denying any part of it is the guaranteed way to continue to repeat stored patterns.

In the personal development world which I was a big part of in my past chapters you are taught that any painful experience is only painful for as long as you hold on to the hurt, and that for as long as you tell the "story," you stay a victim to the experience and will stay stuck. So you get told to "change the story," just "let go" of the emotions attached to it, and "think positive" or "focus on where you want to go."

But what happens when you struggle to get beyond the emotions of significant events? Some events take years to get beyond. The loss of a child or violent abuse or the diagnosis of a life-threatening illness. It's easy to feel like a failure for allowing yourself to go into "being a victim" and think you *should* just be letting go and moving on. For people who have done loads of personal development, there is shame attached to going into any kind of "victim mode" also because of the judgement from a large component of the community who are quick to remind you that you're being a victim or in a victim mentality.

But I want to challenge this thinking …

Are we actually being victims? Really?

I got to experience a great deal of what is professionally called "trauma" in the last few years. Losing my sister, a physical system shut down, and domestic violence leaving me with PTSD, to name a few of the big ones, have come with a large amount of emotional content. These have been harder to get on top of because there has been so much to feel through them. Many layers to face and release both mentally, physically, energetically and emotionally.

Here is the problem …

*When we refuse to "be the victim," we disconnect from the reality of the situation and we deny the fullness of the emotions present, which means complete integration and healing is not possible.*

You can't fully integrate something that you deny exists and that you won't give the space to be acknowledged, felt, and expressed in its rawness. If one is to become whole again it's important to **not** deny what happened, nor to minimise the trauma and the emotions that come with it.

So often those around us just want us to move on, because it triggers their stuff too much or they are in fear for us or just plain selfish.

What if we were to reframe the moments where the realness of the situation is being expressed and felt as being "human" instead of being "a victim"?

I give you complete permission to express how you **really** feel and what you **really** think about what happened to you, even if it's not "constructive" or even rational! How freeing is that? It is liberating to be free to express true emotions in that instance.

No shame, no need to even be mature about it, just raw emotion and thoughts expressed. This is healthy! Let me caveat that by saying they are best expressed in a space by yourself or with a trusted friend or supporter who can hold the space for you to express it without judgement or need to take non-constructive action. Find someone who will allow you to be brutally human! I am blessed to have a few people in my life who can actively be present to allow me to go there. Those chats often end in tears and then laughter. And always with open love expressed. So very healing.

What if you were taught how to fully embrace and love that part of you that got hurt, that is grieving, that is angry, that made mistakes or should have done/known better, and whatever else it's feeling. Not shaming it into submission or denying these emotions are allowed to be there. There is so much shame around trauma in this world that is not being healed and integrated because people are trying not to "be the victim"; it's insanity!

The reality of the situation is that the human was the victim in that moment and it needs to be acknowledged and loved through its pain! Expressing it in raw form doesn't mean we stay there and constantly blame others, but we can be human **and** hold others accountable or hold a new boundary. Victims don't do that. Humans do.

When you go through the reinvention process you'll be getting really honest and vulnerable, giving yourself the necessary time and space to fully integrate all the raw emotional content that's previously been denied or that you have judged or felt shame around feeling. It's time for you to truly become whole because that's where the power to have the life you want is waiting.

**Heal the human. Heal the community. Heal the world. Reinvention is the key.**

Full acknowledgement is essential, full honesty and a real facing off with yourself in the mirror is required. It's up to you! In the Human Reinvention Formula I will show you the process to do this fully!

Your story is significant and you have complete permission to own it,
You matter,
You mean something,
You are allowed to be sad, mad, lost, and confused,
You are beautifully human!

Make sure you take the time to give yourself full acknowledgement.

Remove all shaming and judgement around your story and observe the judgement you may have taken on from others. Turn your story of hardship into a powerful strength but only after it has been acknowledged fully.

Give yourself time, as much time as you need, not the time others need you to process in but your own divine experience of time; be brutally honest with yourself, not playing up or playing down the truth. Do not feel ashamed of any part of your story, even the greatest mistakes of all! This is the only way to be free of them! Take full responsibility for your part in your story—but never someone else's. You are not responsible for how others think, feel, or interpret you. Do not take responsibility for others' failures, decisions, mistakes, or poor behaviour. Be as human as you can, accept your uniqueness, your strengths and your weaknesses, and expect others to accept you as you are! Ha! A simple feat, well not really!

When we think we rule the world, when we strive to be unstoppable or invincible, we miss critical parts of the human experience. I have operated in a superwoman position for years and it caused me enormous struggle trying to maintain a sense of perfection, high standards, and a high performing life.

Today I accept my limitations as a human and accept the possibilities as my whole self!

122

One of the most confusing times of my whole adventure was acceptance, this part is where my reinvention really took me to new heights and new depths all at once!

## Why Would You Engage With the Human Reinvention Formula?

You are a powerful human being and you have experienced either previously or recently a major need to evaluate life for the purpose of reinvention. Things are not how you desired them to be and you recognise that to truly reinvent then you need to go to places you have not been before or even adopt a new way of shifting gears so life does look different in many areas.

Your wealth vehicle might be struggling either through overworking or not receiving the remuneration you deserve. You may find yourself in a model of wealth that is no longer sustainable with the stage of life you're entering. You might be tired doing what you have always done and need a new perspective. The model you chose may not be in your area of strengths. You may be failing at a model and it's time to be courageous and brave and do something fresh and new.

After creating the Mpowered Personal Profile which became the Wealth Performance Profile in 2011, I became an expert in the analysis of alignment to wealth strategies. I had studied psychotherapy and multiple modalities for human transformation and created the profile that supported the transformation of thousands of people. I was able to profile people based on personality, temperament, and beliefs and be able to align wealth strategies to behaviours. Most of all for years I worked with individuals to correct and strengthen weaknesses around wealth creation.

I saw so many extraordinary transformations in the areas of abundance and wealth flow that I am a great believer in the potential of human beings, but there must be a process of defining alignment. Without this I see so many attempt strategies with little result. I am driven to deliver this formula to you in a way that can build your confidence in wealth building again. And show you ways to make informed choices so your ability to create wealth is in flow and sustainable.

It's not too late; you may feel tired, burnt from strategies that did not work for you. You may have trusted people to deliver a strategy and it didn't match what you invested. Whatever your scenario, I beg you not to give up!

Had I given up on my work in the field of human transformation I would have never found the joy I to this day experience when I am able to demonstrate how one transitions through this life to be able to massively up-level income.

*"If I can go from $43 to $50K a month in only nine months after major trauma then anything really is possible. I just had to reinvent myself in the process and find new ways of being in my genius. I had to open my mind up fully"*

We all have a genius if you believe this or not. We all have a path to walk, and not everyone wants business to be the be all and end of your life, but you want the freedom. So you must choose wisely. And it is a delicate selection process. I know these strategies so well, I have invested in so many and I can see now in my own experience why some did not work for me. They just were not in my natural flow. So I return to a field that is my calling then suddenly it flows again. But it takes boldness to be honest enough with yourself to question which pathway is aligned. I say don't bother if you cannot feel alignment on some level as then you may get spat out and waste valuable time. Slow down to allow yourself to align and see what the next steps are. I believe that a much higher force than us ensures we end up in alignment as an end phase and we get tested to show us where we are not aligned.

Your structure for fulfilling your personal needs also may need attention, no doubt. I have only witnessed real shifts in humans when they take the time to understand what their needs really are. Unapologetically living the life that your soul yearns for. For this to become a reality we need to understand patterning and disrupt previous ways of being. Then we can do the upgrade! So many head straight to the upgrade thinking it's the next stage but simply repeat similar patterning.

My understanding of energy management has shifted dramatically throughout my reinventions. Before I thought energy was about exertion, how much I could pour into things. How active I was physically and how much energy I could give to others. I was a massive energy ball machine with no boundaries; I would pour it into everything and with a younger body and innocence I would just keep going. I was the example of full on; I loved fully, gave everything, and would wear myself out on all levels. I actually loved that period, to be honest, it was so free-spirited and alive but it was not sustainable through the different stages of life.

Through life I began to recognise that to manage my energy was far more than the physical type. I developed a strong empathic side and my spiritual sensitivity was insanely high on tap. I would go far beyond my physical capacity and then crash and burn.

The last parts of my recent physical reinvention have given me a whole new understanding of energy for me. It was time to slow down my energy powers, ground them, and begin to rebuild partnerships between the physical and energetic spirit-filled energy.

This has been the hardest part of all. A complete shift in gears to a calm, slow, and completely present energy. What I have found is such a deep ability to manifest and create that is beyond what I have ever experienced before.

You may have noticed you are playing in a lone wolf position and doing the strong person reality. You may have changed your environment or relationships may be released and you are upleveling, therefore finding yourself on this journey alone. Sometimes it can be a highly fuelled and deeply transformative time but beware how long you choose to stay in that stage. I personally have experienced having stayed in my solo stage for too long in both business and socially. It has stalled my growth without a doubt. As I have grown I am able to gauge when it is time to establish new relationships and when it is time to be inwards. I have spent time alone for years ensuring I heal fully.

The power of community is not to be underestimated and to choose this consciously is an incredible process. To also learn to release from communities or relationships when they no longer serve your highest good is quite a learning process too. It's not about rejecting them, it's about accepting what you need next.

If the flow of giving and receiving is not aligned for you it may be time to reinvent this part of your world. You may be a major giver but your cup might be empty. You may contribute to your family and friends and rarely receive back. You may give to charities and give time or money even when you may not have it. You may feel depleted by this imbalance but martyrdom is built into your psyche. This has been a big part of my old story, giving so much to so many people but unable to really trust in receiving until disaster struck. The gifts of much of my traumatic experiences is the incredible angels who appeared and taught me to receive. Incredible angels that appeared and rarely the people I expected.

You may have become complacent about charitable giving and not know there is another way. With the model of social enterprise now you can give and receive at the same time. Exciting times.

## What Is the Human Reinvention Formula?

The human reinvention formula is a process I founded to help me move through some of the most confusing and painful stages in life. I have used it over and over again and bounced into a new levels rapidly. So it is my pleasure to share it with you so you may experience enormous wealth, self-insight, energy, community support, and contribution.

So let's UNPACK the formula!

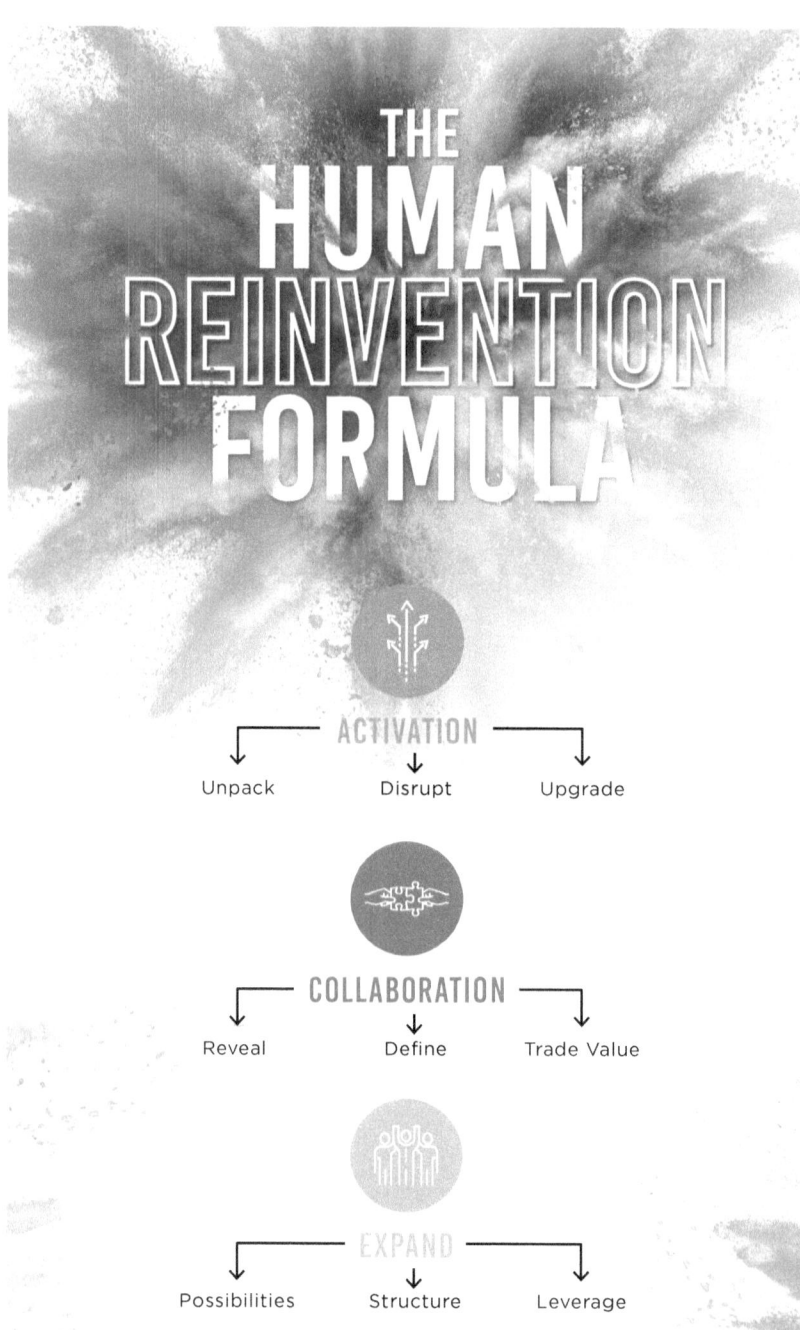

Over the next chapters I will run through the formula and create opportunities for you to actively begin implementation at each stage. Join our community online through our website www.miamunro.com so you can be supported by other people like you who are choosing to reinvent themselves.

If you need further support then we offer a range of opportunities to engage deeper. You will be supported when you reach out!

# CHAPTER 7

# STAGE 1—ACTIVATION

This is our shake-up stage where all stagnant or lodged parts can be loosened up and have the chance of being expanded out. This may have already begun for you in the form of illness, change of work, loss of something, or some life event. For many this is an unexpected shake-up and it is so important to listen here. Not palm it off to some uncontrollable moment in life. Everything is connected on some level.

This stage is the part many miss out on completing because they do not own the story or event and blame others for it. Missing the critical juicy stuff within it. What happens next is you will continue doing what you have always done and repeat patterns and realities without strengthening and growing. This is how trauma is passed on and on through generations because the work to release and resolve it has not been completed. I am deeply motivated to see trauma resolved so humanity can elevate collectively. I have a deep and personal motivation to commit myself to this work. One for my own embodiment of humanness and the creation of a life that is in sync and full of joy but also because I have been affected greatly by others' traumas and in some instances as I have already shared really hurt by the unconscious behaviours of others. This is not to say that I am not human and no doubt have also created trauma too. It's time to stop patterns and become a race of wide-awake humans who operate from a conscious position. It's time for us to thrive! A new world comes from the reinvention of human beings into far more conscious and deliberate decision-making machines.

There are three parts within the stage of Activation

1. Unpack
2. Disrupt
3. Upgrade

Let's break these down for you now and you can begin to work on each stage. Resources are referred to at the back of the book and FREE resources can be accessed through our website www.miamunro.com.

# Unpack

*"It takes courage to unpack your business and life to see the pathway it will actually take you on. Disrupting our lives, our businesses, and even industries requires deep diving to understand the core restrictions and opportunities to be awakened. When you upgrade your blueprint something indescribable occurs when energy and forces beyond yourself enter to guide you forth. An activated leader need not battle or fight for what they need, an integrated approach brings about new openings"*

*MIA MUNRO*

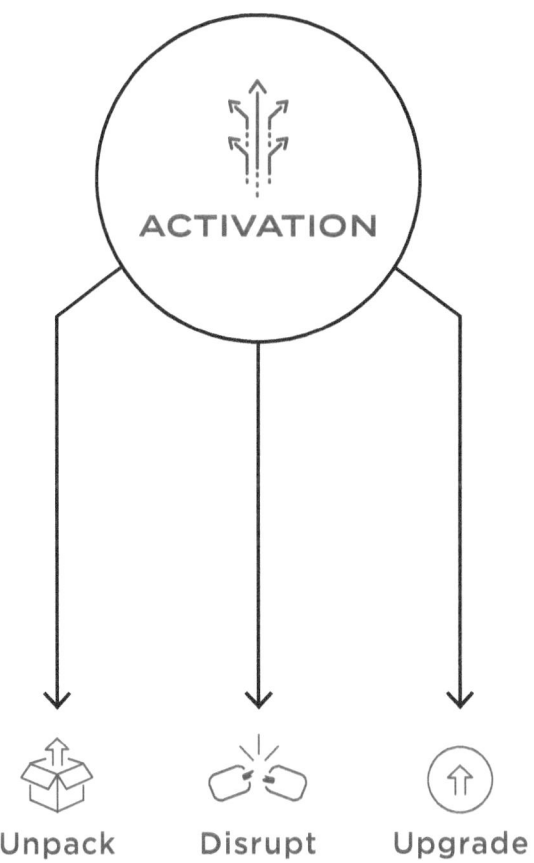

To unpack one's life is to see it truthfully without distraction or delusion. We often stand in a position or role and separate the essence of who we are with the work we need to do.

The old saying "Leave your personal life at the door" is far from a realistic or acceptable approach to a whole life. You are your whole life and therefore the integration of all parts without separation. To UNPACK we need courage to see what we have chosen to ignore, to shine a mirror up and gracefully find some new acceptance around it.

We need to look beneath the obvious! Not get stuck in our pain but move through it fully.

We need to UNPACK fully our experiences to allow for the RELEASE of references that simply mask the actual wounding which is blocking your way forward.

Dipping our toes in deeper reveals more truth and allows for progress forward.

The next stage after unpacking is laying out possible ways you are viewing your challenge and actively DISRUPT THEM! Put yourself in another's shoes and see the situation from a completely different perspective. Dissociate from it to be able to see through it.

Challenging your own stories or dialogue can be confronting but also liberating!

See how we move shame and blame to deception, a much deeper theme to uncover and resolve!

# Unpack—Simple Activities to Get You Started

To begin ...

1. On review of your current experience of life what area needs the MOST attention right now? e.g. Wealth, Self, Energy, Community, Contribution
2. What restrictions do you see are in place around this area of life right now?
3. What three themes come to mind when you relate to your MOST recent challenge area?
4. What are your first thoughts around these themes?
5. What do you need most in the short, medium, and long term around this area?

This is the UNPACKING PHASE only—No need for perfectionism, just trust what comes out. Of course if there are more themes, keep writing! If you have done exercises like this before I ask you to swipe the slate clear and trust in this process.

Let me show you some examples:

In 2011, I received one of those calls that changes everything. I was at a café with a team member enjoying a yummy piece of cake and a coffee. It was 5 p.m. on a Friday and I was reflecting on some concerns I was having with my business partners. I had been feeling high levels of stress as I felt my company was at risk and my business partnership was not in flow. I was confused about how to move forward. My trust was getting lower every day and I lacked the previous business and financial experience to know what to do.

I knew something had to change. I was burnt out from continuously speaking at events, being the CEO, mentor, and all the other roles one operates in a startup company. The phone call brought news that said we were going into voluntary liquidation. No mention of this prior and no option for me to make my own informed decision. I felt a rise of anger and a determination to not be "done over" and the battle began.

I felt devastated, my team lost their jobs with little warning and my business partners tried to steal my Intellectual Property. I felt victimised, a failure, and out of my depth. Shame, pain, and fear engulfed me. My baby (my business that I created) was dead in an instance. I didn't realise how attached I had become to it and serving our clients. How could the thousands of hours of work and dedication result in a sudden death to the business right before I was able to even consider on-selling the business which was our goal.

## Here is an example after DOING this exercise:

**On review of your current experience of life what area needs the MOST attention right now?** e.g. Wealth. Self, Energy, Community, Contribution

- ○ Wealth Flow

**What restrictions do you see are in place around this area of life right now?**

- ○ Energy to manage change
- ○ Impact on my team
- ○ Feeling deep in distrust and uncertainty

**What three themes come to mind when you relate to your MOST recent challenge area?**

- ○ Blame, shame, victim
- ○ Loss of control of my future
- ○ Failure and loss

## What are your first thoughts around these themes?

- I wanted to blame, shame, and collapse into victim. And this is a very normal, human response.

- I collapsed into a spiralling feeling of a loss of control. Feeling terrible for my team and their loss. I focused on loss of control and used all energy to regain control, missing this very important human emotion of guilt.

- The failure and loss of that company and impact on my team. This is normal no doubt but I was missing the deep stored loss of belief in my ability to grow an empire again. Stalling my life's work. And contributing to exhaustion.

## What do you need most in the short, medium and long term around this area?

- A plan to navigate through the next three steps I need to take
- Some control over my future
- A sense of certainty that I won't lose everything

What a relief to be able to NAME the suffering in the first instance. Remember this is pre - disruption so we often act on our initial responses when in fact if we slow down to speed up our actions may be far more measured and create new outcomes. You should find this a relief to download this onto paper but I appreciate it may still be fuelled with pain, anger, or loss.

Next stage is disruption, the part that so often gets missed and can result in a negative human experience becoming stored in the body until it is unlocked, often not when we need! We do not want this, disrupting as we go allows for a smoother transition and integration.

# Disrupt

Disruption is a common phrase used in business but rarely in life. Are we prepared to disrupt our own life?

It is rare to meet or witness a true disruptor who is not prepared to go beyond the norm and is able to operate effectively there. Be it pioneering a new construct, building a new technology, activating a new community or tribe, breaking through in a new science, or a personal breakthrough. It takes a need to activate a desire, then an urgency to look into old paradigms and witness what is no longer working for you, at this place and at this time. And as we evaluate the old paradigms it can often bring about frustration or even confusion. Once you are expanded, it is not possible to contract to old ways. The focus is to be courageous and disrupt your own thoughts, your current reality, and the way it translates into your life, business, and community.

We need to UNPACK our experiences fully to allow for the RELEASE of references that simply mask the actual wounding. Dipping our toes in deeper reveals more truth and allows for progress forward.

The next stage after unpacking is laying out possible ways you are viewing your challenge and actively DISRUPT THEM! Challenging your own stories or dialogue can be confronting but also liberating! See how we move from shame and blame in my next example to deception which is a much deeper theme which can unlock the potential old dysfunction in relationships!

# Disrupt—Simple Activities to Get You Started

To begin …

1. Review your three themes and ask yourself—Are these real and serving my highest good?
2. Go inwards and notice what themes you initially stated and observe what sits just under them. What is beneath your initial thoughts or feelings? Consider ideas, try them on. Trust yourself with what comes up.
3. Now disrupt the old themes and state them with confidence.
4. What do these new themes give you?
5. What evidence do you have to know that these will allow you to release any old trauma around them? I call this the "evidence board" and access it when I really need to remember progress.

Allow your deeper insight and wisdom to come through—TRUST yourself here! Review my examples and IMAGINE you know. Then close your eyes and sense into if these are true for you! At this stage all we are doing is DISRUPTING THEM!

Disruption is all about challenging past paradigms and beliefs. Seeing if they hold true to you anymore or can they be released? What evidence can you see to shape a new reality? What wisdom has life just given you?

## Let me show you some examples:

### Review your three initial themes that you unpacked and ask yourself—Are these real and serving my highest good?

- Blame, shame, victim
- Loss of control of my future
- Failure and loss

*"NO WAY! I feel disempowered"*

**Go inwards and notice what themes you initially stated and observe what sits just under them. What is beneath your initial thoughts or feelings?**

- Blame, shame, victim to DECEPTION

  With time I identified a pattern which ran deeper— Deception. This was a theme that would play out in many areas of my life as it was never resolved at this time. The source of this began very young in life.

  Loss of control of my future to GUILT

  Years later it was "guilt" I carried most and a deep sense of failing those I loved most. I focused on loss of control and used all energy to regain control, missing this very important human emotion of guilt. Carrying the burden of guilt affected many reinventions in my businesses. I feared building teams again and let them down. This stalled business growth.

- Failure and loss to LACK OF SELF-BELIEF

  I was missing the deep stored loss of belief in my ability to grow an empire again. Stalling my life's work. And contributing to exhaustion. This loss of self-belief rippled through my whole life in many forms.

**Now disrupt the old themes and state them with confidence**

- What holds true for me is that I have experienced a sense of Deception. I feel guilty that I thought I had let my team down. I had missed the fraudulent behaviour and red flags. I had a strong lack of self-belief as this was my first big company and fear I could ever build one again.

**What do these new themes give you?**

- I recognise that I did not have to hold off for many years to launch back into the market. Healing these wounds allows me to now forgive myself fully and let it go. I do not take responsibility for the behaviour of my business partners. I am not responsible for the path my team followed and I am aware they also were opened to learnings too. There was no failure, just an opportunity to learn, strengthen, and uplevel. I can launch into the market again knowing I have learned valuable lessons about business. I can see the evidence of how incredible that company was and how I put my heart into it. I did my very best and next time comes with greater wisdom.

**What evidence do you have to know that these insights will allow you to release any old trauma around them?**

- I can own my fears, stand strong in my conviction and take strides to expand into a more powerful business owner. I relaunch myself in a new way with confidence and belief.

The disruption process is critical and you can run it through many areas of your life to gain shifts and perspectives. Integration is what comes next and the upgrade.

I could have placed all my focus on WEALTH when in fact SELF needed the MOST work! If we do not focus on the deeper area, we may miss the greatest opportunities for upgrade!

# Upgrade

*"A version upgrade is an opportunity to examine the depths of you, beyond ego to locate your soul's desires to reinvent yourself. It stimulates conscious decision making and activates the fulfilment of needs. Therefore creating a business or life that is fully integrated, authentic, and congruent"*

*MIA MUNRO*

After unpacking and disrupting you can begin to look at the upgrade you need to be able to collaborate and expand effectively.

We need to consider what your new human reinvention design plan may become. There are no two the same and yet so many leaders look to model others. You are a unique individual who needs a unique plan. Once you design this fully everything shifts!

## Upgrade—Simple Activities to Get You Started

Begin by completing the Activation Map. This asks you a series of questions in detail for you to be able to envision a new pathway. This Activation Map is one tool that is used to allow you to expand deeper into your internal motivators and triggers. It can provide evidence of your true needs and visions.

Here are a series of questions that will give you information for your activation map.

1. What do you stand against? **WHAT INFURIATES YOU?** This is an opportunity to tap into that which aggravates you, frustrates you, and stimulates you to want to do something.

2. What do you stand for? **TRANSLATE WHAT INFURIATES YOU INTO WHAT WILL EMPOWER YOU!** Write freely without too much analysis. At this stage it is best not to think too much, just get this down on paper. State your vision. What do you want to see, experience, and know in your future? Imagine a new world without the struggle you may face. What would that look like?

3. What do you need? What needs do you have that are not being met, e.g. financial support, connection, physical energy, opportunities?

4. For each need, what is missing? List what is missing and be brutally honest with yourself. Are these excuses to not move forward or do they feel real and constricting? Write these out, as many as your mind can create.

5. What resources do you need to source? What do you need access to, e.g. time, money, opportunities or support?

6. What impact would receiving these resources make right now?

7. How committed are you to impacting your own world? On a scale of 1 – 5 what level of commitment are you at?

8. Who could help you right now?

9. What are the real limitations you can see?

10. What needs to occur next?

You can download the FREE template to fill in. This is located at our website www.miamunro.com.

Next, summarise for the area that needs most of your focus right now, often not the original focus area.

Create a simple 1, 2, 3 clarity list for this area. Chunk it down so your mind can grasp the new pathway!

Now create a 1, 2, 3 ACTION LIST that will allow you to begin to expand from this place with ease and grace.

In the online community you will see other reinvention tools such as:

- How to create your personal manifesto and creed
- Templates for your Activation Map and design plan
- Active meditations for busy minds

You can download these for FREE now at www.miamunro.com

# CHAPTER 8

# STAGE 2—COLLABORATION

*"To be resourceful one must recognise the resources available to them. A lack of insight into these powerful gems can hinder any leader from attracting in the bigger resources required to activate, disrupt, and serve through their business. So we must reveal, define, build, and trade these valuable assets as a normal part of our daily structure. When this is activated a powerful wealth can be built. A wealth beyond money, a sustainable wealth that impacts the very nature of humanity"*

*MIA MUNRO*

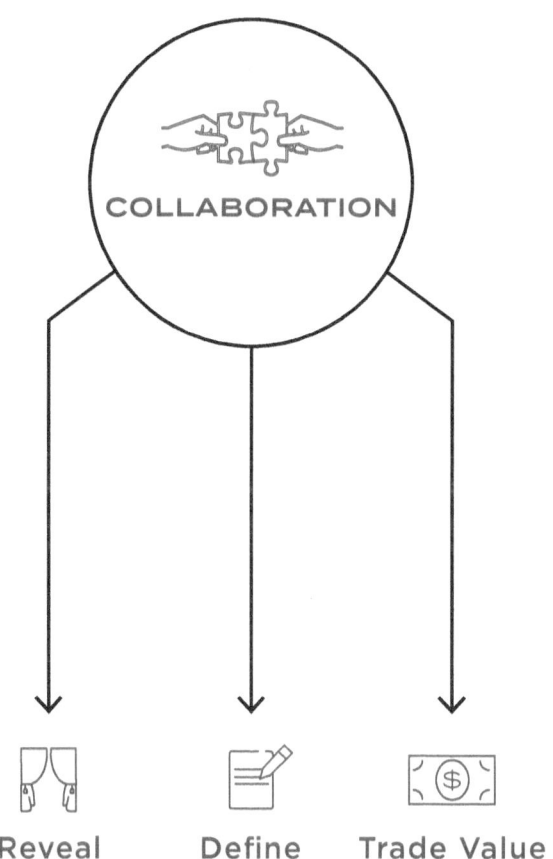

We now move in to Stage 2 of the formula and begin to look into our environment and how we work within it. How we relate to others and how we work to create a greater, more effective reality. Activation is a solo ride initially but now we move from "I—Egocentric" to "US—Ethnocentric" then into "WE—World centric" in Stage 3.

Who we choose to be surrounded with does impact our reality.

The success-driven, wealth-focused world promotes you are the net worth of the five people you hang around with and although I do agree with this as a concept it is missing important factors to be balanced. If you surround yourself with high achievers all making money and that is their greatest focus in life you will often all then face exhaustion together at the same time, or loss of money. It also lacks major qualities in humans too. When it comes to the upgrade of wealth yes, it is essential to surround yourself with those whom you can learn from. But some of my greatest teachers and relationships in life have been what I call "unlikely humans." People who come from completely different industries and life experiences. This is where I have grown exponentially.

During many of my reinvention chapters, I have chosen to change environments to give me  breadth-of-life experiences. Living in Indonesia for example opened me up in a big way to a different pace of life. It showed how living in paradise and working half days was an essential ingredient for my success. I have hardly worked more than half a day to half a week in years. In fact, over the last 15 years I have lived in diverse communities and my greatest life growth has come from these places.

Different cultures have given me gifts the Western culture misses. Different languages have given me different ways to express myself. And different food has given me a deep appreciation of amazing food.

So how rich is our life, not meaning rich as in money but as in enriched with joy, wild experiences, and deep love?

This stage is about revealing your riches, the gems in your life that perhaps you are not consciously giving energy to. The resources that could help you uplevel so fast. It's something I have fallen into throughout each stage out of necessity but I now deliberately access at each stage. Let's start collaborating, but in a true sense of the word.

## Reveal (Resources)

We rarely bring light to the value of resources around us and rarely realise just how rich we are. We are in search for what we do not have. What if we searched within what we have? This reveal stage is essential to uncover your value and the value of those you choose to share your time with. Your value is far grander than just your business, money, or your profile. Your value is not measured or assessed for what it can really give you. But when uncovered and expressed it then becomes something that can be exchanged with others, and watch life expand then!

Our value should be defined by us but is often depleted by others or old societal constructs. I have seen this many times. We exist in a world that assesses what is valuable according to a set of outdated rules or reference points. When we look from a different perspective much can be revealed. We can gain an empowered approach to our life when we own our value and respect the values of others.

So let's begin to look back on your life themes so far and decide which resources could be perceived as valuable.

Brainstorm a list of people, places, things, moments, experiences, skills, evidence of impact ...

Value for one can be different for another, e.g. *A working mother may value the opportunity to access digital marketing experience of another and yet be unsure of what value they can exchange. To the person with digital marketing exchanging the skills a mother possesses could be the magic for their ability to build productivity.* This is a basic example, there are no limits.

We need to delve deeply into these to reveal opportunities perhaps unseen before. And create a strategic plan to engage more specific resources for your expansion. This can unlock enormous wealth doorways that will enhance your reinvention process. We can look at time capsules and witness the power of time, define your financial ceilings, and find evidence which can indicate openings. This can be a profound process that can be supported by someone acting as your guide through this process. But to get started ...

## Reveal—Simple Activities to Get You Started

Begin by revealing the resources you currently have in your life, such as money, time, network, skills, experiences, potential collaborators, and energy.

Here are some examples:

WEALTH BUILDING SKILLS: professional training, career, sales or marketing ability, online, networking, administration, creation, writer, speaker

SELF: silence, space, love and support, meditation, education, time, environments

ENERGY BUILDING RESOURCES: programmes, groups, supplements, health protocols, practitioners, practices

COMMUNITY: business connections, family connections, sport or exercise clubs, wellness groups, social groups, mentors, teachers, healers, doctors

CONTRIBUTION: charities, social enterprises, donor pro-grammes, international travel, paying it forward

Can you notice any forms of blocks around seeing your value?

Can you see any invisible ceilings around what is possible for you right now? I have experienced this frequently in my career after a major turning point; I would often plummet into a lower financial ceiling for some time before building it back up again.

So let's say in my business I was able to bring in $10k a month in consulting fees. There was a point where I could not expand above this. It required me to do some wealth mindset work to expand up into the $20k and beyond. Having a financial ceiling is real and most traditional jobs have ceilings which is why I would say I am unemployable as it would risk me collapsing my financial ceiling. So my value was blocked by my belief of what was possible. Something we do not want to limit your next stages.

## Ceiling of Possibility

What do you believe is your current financial ceiling? The amount of money you tend to attract in and even if it drops it seems to go back to the same level? Can you imagine yourself expanding beyond this? Is it something you need to do? If you begin a new wealth venture without consciousness around this ceiling then you may sabotage over and over again the behaviours that keep you there. Something to be very aware of.

What about your self value? Your belief in what you can give to the world? Does this have a ceiling or level in which it is capped?

Get clear on this to get started; we just need you to reveal your opportunities for now and your current ceiling. We can expand later.

# Define (Your People)

Are you clear who your people are and their roles? Have you created a structure to support a trust-based community? Who is in and who is out? (done respectfully always)

How would you prefer to relate in the future, what values would they operate from?

For me, I looked into the value of the people around me. For me it was a sensing activity; who did I feel uplifted with and who drained my energy consistently? Because energy has become such an important factor. That is not to say I choose people based on always feeling good for that would be to avoid conflict and project a superficial reality of positiveness, the very construct I needed to remove.

I remember one woman in one community I was part of, I always felt a strong ego energy from her. My past teachings said look in the mirror first so I evaluated myself and I felt really at peace. She was always secretive in her business ideas and yet I would share freely which indicated a real lack of trust from within her. And also a real sense of not being comfortable being honest. I stuck with her for some time as she was a spiritual teacher but over time it became clear who she was and where she was operating from. This would never serve my soul.

When I was facing decisions about changing environments it was her behaviour that threw me most of all. She was exactly what I had perceived her to be. I just had not trusted myself in my decision around that relationship. She was not operating from the same place of openness, and that will never allow a relationship to thrive. Egoic teachers can be difficult ones, maybe that was even me before I found humility, my good friend. Not to judge anyone to be right or wrong just to notice if it serves us. If not we have a choice to release without guilt. We get to choose who will be in our environment.

It is okay to make strong choices around your people and absolutely trust your intuition. My do-gooder program needed some conditioning in this area!

Another example is a woman I knew in Sydney who made a bold comment one day about the changes I had made in the communities I was part of. Her judgement was that there was something wrong with me because I chose to move through and release relationships that no longer served me. I loved that opportunity to strengthen my own belief in trusting myself.

Communities or relationships that are not functional are often based on lies or deception and these rarely can work. I choose more open-hearted relationships with maturity and compassion for resolving all challenges. You can choose too.

Returning to the wealth arena was an interesting ride for me too. I had been on stages and supported great change in the past but I had also been surrounded by speakers and business owners who blatantly lie often in marketing and fool new clients. So I had to use pure discernment when returning to the industry recently. To block an industry was not smart but to engage in it with a clearer definition of integrity was my decision. I chose partners I trusted who run epic companies to ensure my time with them was aligned with my values. If there is a hint it is not, it becomes an opportunity to upgrade.

We do not need to hold all the same beliefs with our communities, just a conscious alignment of values is necessary. My filter was to bring in a diverse group of incredibly conscious human beings, people operating with high integrity, self-responsibility, and an openness to what is possible.

It is time to deliberately choose your people now.

# Define—Simple Activities to Get You Started

This part can begin as you are entering a new reinvention period but it's okay if it changes as you emerge more fully on the other side.

Define your future people and how they align to your reinvention:

1. Unpack who is in your network now and their value. Who are they and what value do they bring to your life from a wealth, self, energy, community, and contribution perspective?
2. Redefine the people aligned to your next stages. Who do you need in your next stages to support your expansion or to begin to collaborate with? As I was wanting to bring in more self-expression I began to seek out new musically aligned connections so I could expand into new areas.
3. Notice the possible stages of rebuild for you. What is missing in your connections and what value do you need?
4. What are the critical Roles required for each area but in particular the area of most focus right now? Here are some examples:

   *A/ WEALTH—Online wealth builders, investors, advisors, mentors*

   *B/ SELF—Different philosophies, people living alternative lifestyles,*

   *C/ ENERGY—New modalities for energy creation*

   *D/ COMMUNITY—New tribes locally, nationally, and globally*

   *E/CONTRIBUTION—Possible new alignments to projects*

# Build and Trade (Your Sustainable Circle)

To begin, some of you may find you are starting all over again, whilst others will remain in some communities but release others. Relationships may begin to change deliberately and your new circle of support, influences, and expansion is beginning to take shape.

So let me explain these concepts for you:

*To Build means to actively invest energy into the creation of new relationships that support your highest good.*

*To Trade is to present your value to another and accept their value too. In most cases finding a mutual alignment in something of importance to you both that assists in growth.*

*Your Sustainable Circle becomes your tribe of whom are consciously chosen to allow for giving and receiving to be activated to produce outcomes of value that support your reinvention.*

When you are ready to build and then trade value with your new deliberately chosen people, the most important focus is ownership of your personal value. This is not simply business skills, money, or time but the elements that you choose to exchange that hold value to another.

As humans we often do not see our true value in the growth experienced through being a parent, for example. A person who has travelled multiple countries may not see the value of the growth that has come from working or connecting within different cultures or speaking different languages.

*"True personal value is the sum of all your life experiences and those leaders who have embraced their value are able to trade it with ease"*

When your value is defined we tap into what it is you're prepared to trade; this brings into alignment your use of time, energy, and financial resources. So often we trade something that holds a higher value to them. But it does not serve you. It can be done out of obligation or conditioning. The martyr does this often. This is not sustainable and leads to burnout, health issues, relationships breakups, and a lack of fulfilment.

We are either trading or paying for something. If it is not mutually beneficial then it's an act of kindness which of course is so essential in life if balanced or you are allowing yourself to be used. We do this sometimes to feel a higher sense of self-worth. But it rarely ends up that way in the long run.

How you build your circle is how you will gain support and experience expansion. How you trade is how you choose to live, your lifestyle, your relationships, the impact you have on others, and your ability to stay in the game of life with joy and energy!

## Build and Trade—Simple Activities to Get You Started

Here we want you to define your needs. What do you need to build in order to upgrade your circle and support systems? What is your personal value? What are you prepared to trade?

1. What is your greatest need right now?
2. What people do you need most right now to help or support?
3. What is your personal value, the parts of you that are magnificent?
4. What could you trade with another to build an effective new relationship?
5. When will you know these are your people?

# CHAPTER 9

# STAGE 3—EXPANSION

*"Creating expansion comes with pain and pleasure. With the Human Reinvention Formula you can open up possibilities that will result in pleasure, abundance, and expansion. But we must open up, structure for growth, and leverage for the ultimate experience. Challenge becomes our friend and we gain so much when this becomes the norm of the human experience"*

*MIA MUNRO*

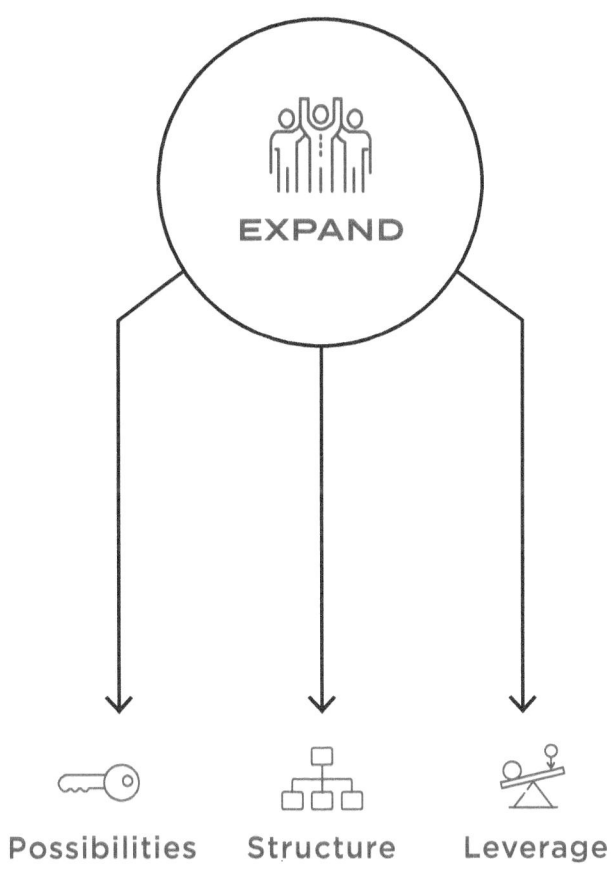

Expansion is the stunning gift at the end of this ride of a lifetime! It is your birthright!

New possibilities are birthed here, structures to support ongoing growth are in place, and you have a chance to leverage opportunities. This is my all-time favorite part because this is where seeds are planted and roots grow. Sometimes we even see a sprout of new growth every day. We then build the strength in our plant to weather the next chapters of life! And fertilise it daily!

## OPEN to New Possibilities

Opening up to a more abundant experience where time, money, and impact is more aligned to your core needs becomes a wonderful reward once integration had occurred. Fulfilment, joy, and a holistic experience is achieved and the ripple effect can be grand.

When we look at opening up we can consider this from three perspectives:

Self (Egocentric)—Your own internal world,

Others (Ethnocentric)—Other people's world, and

World (World centric)—A global world. This creates a depth of insight that expands the riches of life rapidly.

You may currently be living in an area that has served you for many years, but you are starting to challenge seeing a future there. You may be in a career that you trained hard for but you are beginning to question doing this for the next 10 years. Your relationship may be dying and you know to allow it to keep on the same path would create separation. It may need a shake-up. You may be ready to live in a new country or learn a new language. You may know it's time to leave the world of an employee and study a new home-based business with new mentors?

Whatever you feel disgruntled about you can now begin to entertain new possibilities. Start by dreaming fully again without boundaries or limitations. Just imagine what life could be like.

Think about your needs by acknowledging the changes in your life and what needs to shift with it. What passions were left behind due to external influences?

I had a dream to sing sweet music and move people. To activate people's truth through the vibration of sound. I trained as a young person and sung for many years. But after being shut down I lost my passion. I didn't want to become a mass-produced singer who lost her soul.

I knew I needed to still positively impact others so I chose the pathway of speaking. A career I began 15 years ago and now travel and tour with when I choose to. But even though I love speaking so much and it moves people, the real reason I gave up singing was because of the loss of hearing I suddenly experienced in 2004. My right ear shut down to certain tones and I lost so much confidence.

In 2015, I was in Bali and I decided one night to sing again, and the response I received was magical. It was not perfect but I moved people. Activating and moving people deep in their souls is a part of my life's work

Fast forward 2019 and after a profound sound healing I heard the message clearly. You will sing again. Your voice will heal many people. Well, I really wanted to squash this message. For to open to it would mean to have to go into the fear of where my voice was at and experience the real loss of hearing again. I had covered it up for years. Was I too old or too blah blah blah to do this? Of course not but the perceived limitations were real when I listened in silence.

Through this reinvention period, the opportunity appeared. I sang freely and felt the immediate return of the joy of what music brings. It was liberating to allow sound to move through my whole being. The energy that I experienced was beyond anything I had experienced for many years, And I made a decision. I will sing again but this time I will do it my way with my own style and it will heal people. It will bring joy and open hearts; the vibrations of this sound will heal my body and it will heal dis-ease for others. I do not need to know how ... I need to simply open! Watch this space.

Now it's your turn!

## Open—Simple Activities to Get You Started

This exercise expands all areas and allows you to access new doorways perhaps not considered previously. Open up new possibility filters to a high level of abundance, focusing on impact to self, others, and the world.

1. What makes your soul sing? What makes you feel alive?
2. What were you told in younger years you could not do?
3. What limitations do you see? Why is this restricted? What beliefs are playing havoc here?
4. What do you need in your life again? What is missing?
5. What are you going to open to now and begin to allow new thoughts to emerge with?

Now commit to more investigation, this may take time for you. The outcome from opening up to new possibilities is to open to new pathways to build wealth, develop yourself, create energy and vibrations that move you forward, surround you with your new aligned people and community, and that creates a natural embodiment of contribution outwards fulfilling your whole self needs!

Now state boldly a possible pathway knowing it is nto about controlling anything but opening to new parts.

In the next seven days what actions can you take to open this up further so you can feel it and it excites you? Chunking this down is essential. The last thing we want to do is create more separation. Be kind to yourself.

Then step out to 30 days and decide what you need to support this shift. Now imagine three months from now and describe how this would feel. Now three, six, and twelve months from now, what would you be celebrating?

This is not goal setting, or an activity to create perfectionism, expectations, or separation. This is to expand and open new doorways.

## Structure for Expansion

*"Expansion happens on all levels and I found that to create a structure to support this stage means I can ebb and flow with it. As humans we need structure so if we keep it all up in the air then rarely is it a powerful transition. Structure gives us freedom as long as it is coupled with permission to listen to my energetic needs. I am okay and kind to myself when my plan needs to be changed and my structure has to be adjusted according to my needs. I come first!"*

Once your needs are identified you need to map out a strategic expansion plan with appropriate structures in place to support this reinvention. These structures can be financial tracking, self-reflection, energy management, regular connection, tracking of impact, health and energy structures, investment vehicles, time productivity, spiritual time, developing relationships, and whatever you require to support this to be sustainable.

When I was in the midst of my reinvention, my energetic needs were all over the place. I would make plans and almost daily have to change them and I experienced initially a real lack of understanding, especially in the business world. But my energy needs come first so it quickly cleared out the types of people I would be prepared to do business with.

I am grateful for those intolerant people who lacked insight or empathy because it caused me to learn to communicate differently. I had real healing to go through and I had no idea how I would feel one day to the next. Ideally we do go into our cocoon at this time and do the work to heal but so often our circumstances do not match being able to do that.

I did not have children so I had space, but I also lacked daily support. So all situations have their challenges. When I recognised that it was up to me to educate others of my needs, I let go of others' expectations. I created a new conversation that involved sharing how I was, what it meant to me and what it might mean for others. Wow, this was liberating to be surrounded then by people who came for their hearts and understood the complexity of healing crises and the need to ebb and flow.

A structure I set up with friends was in the form of a letter. In business I created meetings to explain my needs and manage expectations. With family I needed to explain how I was feeling and what I needed, including my lack of capacity to help at times. I did not expect anyone to mind read my needs, I created the insight for others. How often do we forget to communicate our needs?

It was the first time I had really shared what I needed without guilt or the pushing or pulling of someone else's expectations. You see, being a high level empath I feel what others are feeling so if they have lots of disappointment I will feel it, but it is not mine to manage. It's a constant check-in process to manage my needs, not theirs!

Accepting your own needs must come first then you can structure those and everyone else around them. Not something I really understood before. This new structure around my relationships was to stay and although some would find it difficult that was their stuff to manage, not mine. I still feel a newbie at this one as if someone needs me or is in pain I want to jump but it's just not possible anymore all the time. The energy crashes showed me that!

I am not sure if those people knew how much I put them before myself, it was so ingrained in me. But it is now in my self-awareness and will allow me to manage my energy so much better than ever. I see so many big-hearted people giving way more than they have and the only option on the other side of that is a crash!

We can access many resources and place structures around all parts of out reinvention . I like to call them clarity structures with enormous flexibility when required. This is not the same as not being accountable. They are built with the insight that you are moving through a reinvention process and may have different needs at this time. We can bring in new funding pathways, new communities, and new experiences of time to expand within. We can break down each part into months so we can understand our main needs. We can screen all activities through our whole self needs. Then enhance and support to increase our productivity and impact.

The sky's the limit of how structures can help you leverage your time and move towards the completion of your reinvention *(well, this version anyway)*. Structure is so important and so is the ability for it to shift and be remodelled as required.

Here is a scenario around a structure that I created for one of my transitions from healing my energetic system, creating new streams of income and tapping into a new community all at once!

I evaluated my needs. For my energetic system I needed both deep rest and stimulation of serotonin levels. I needed positive experiences to look forward to. I needed to add in natural practices that would support this. Each morning I would wake with the sunrise so I could begin the day with a fresh vision. I would sun gaze for a few minutes and mentally decided to clear any feelings that did not serve me. I set an intention for myself. Not forcing myself into positive mantras which were far from where I was at. I allowed emotions to flow, I chose acceptance, allowance to grieve, permission to not be in action, and celebrated even a tiny bit of progress.

This was far more aligned to what most teach. The famous hour of power concept did not serve in this space, I needed a gentler approach.

Next structure was to create a ritual to get hydrated, take my biochemistry supplements and daily cuppa. If I needed coffee I would make it slowly with intention and appreciate the help it gave my body at that time. I did not go into judgement about what I needed to function at that stage and knew I would rise in energy more naturally in the future.

I would fill the room with beautiful music, sit peacefully, and whale watch from the deck for 25 minutes without any access to phones or technology.

It took a while to create this ritual, and I tweaked it many times, but to this day has been the greatest server of my energy and it will always change as I do!

Next was to create a structure around creating additional income. First I needed to choose what pathways were best for this time and aligned to my skill base. I will cover this off in the leverage section. So I had chosen an online model that involved sharing a new and exciting business model and then building and supporting small teams. I had little left in the tank to give out but knew this would support my next stages.

The purpose of this business was to find something to work at home, doing something I found simple and that required a "tap in" approach of energy. And that is what it was. Returning me income within a few weeks made me very happy. I definitely went off plan several times and pulled myself back in. And I did this several times before I found a rhythm that meant I could continue to receive income online whilst writing this book and fulfilling my other needs.

The structure became 30 minutes twice a day I connected out to peeps. I spoke to someone new most days and I supported the team as required. I had found a business that could ebb and flow with my needs, and the mastery to come was to duplicate and sustain that.

Tapping into a new community was the harder one as I just didn't feel great. But to spend several months in insolation was not going to be healthy either. So I created a connection plan to allow me to begin to nurture new relationships. Wow, this one has been outstanding, the ability to be able to build such deep and authentic connections so quickly and hardly head out of my home, bliss. I became clear on whom I wished to attract in, I would then get contacted randomly, often through social media, and I would also send out contacts.

I chose an activity a week I could go to which supported my energetic needs and/or a cafe connection with the view that if I was fatigued it would be rescheduled. And boom, stunning new connections began to emerge, In my past chapter I would have hidden away for months.

I dreamed up local adventures and ticked them off, ensuring they aligned to the new version of me and life began to become enriched again in a new way. One of my favourite recently was swimming with the whales on the Sunshine Coast. I cannot explain the excitement and I squealed unashamedly with joy at such beauty and divinity in these creatures of the sea! A passion I intend to continue with future adventures, swimming with the whales in one of my first homes in the kingdom of Tonga. Ahh, that's another book!

So structure comes from understanding ourselves as human beings, the need for a structure or reference point to our needs. We make the "being" part of high importance and the structure gives us the map! Not the other way around!

I have always been a freedom seeker, hence my life and the way it has been. Structure always felt limiting to me until I experienced the freedom it gave me!

It is very difficult to transition without giving your mind some structure to follow. It is a map only, it is not the absolute experience. And therefore may need to be updated and act as a LIVE map for you to follow!

# Structure—Simple Activities to Get You Started

Now look at the 1, 2, or 3 areas that need your energy and focus— Wealth, Self, Energy, Community, or Contribution.

We want to now create a map. You can do this in an Excel spreadsheet if you need that type of structure or a more creative representation, whatever best aligns to your style. You can access templates in our online community.

For each area we want you to envision progress in a statement. Here is an example:

Wealth—I feel a sense of confidence around my wealth. I open to see new income flowing in and this is allowing me to deeply trust and relax throughout this important reinvention period.

Then state the daily ritual or behaviour that will support that:

- I have a clear direction on how much I choose to bring in new income. I sit on my deck each morning and remember my commitment to this income-producing activity.
- I focus 30 mins x 2 per day on this business.
- I connect via messenger or phone with three new people, conscious of the need to build a new sense of community.
- I acknowledge my genius daily and in doing so remember my brilliance in my chosen area.
- I run my daily budget and acknowledge my adherence to it.

Now, create a visual representation of what this will bring me:

I create an online vision style map with photos of whales, my cats, and a healthy and energetic woman surrounded by loving people. I see my home with beautiful artwork created by people I appreciate. I see strong business partnerships based on balanced masculine and feminine aspects where all parties benefit. It can have on it the simplest of pleasures and also the grandest of ideas.

This goes on a wall, computer, phone, or wherever you can see this daily. It is not a goal list, it is a representation of how you will feel. That is how we create from a why, a need or a desire to feel a certain way. Connection to our emotions manifests and creates possibilities!

This is your start and we can take you beyond here in the online community.

When structure is in place, progress occurs. But we must move away from the old paradigm of structure being a limiting factor. We see so much of that in our society. This is a freedom-creating structure. Have fun creating structures or support your reinvention, and play with them. Allow them to serve you and support your focus.

## Leverage

*"In my recent reinvention, I have experienced the most profound support from within my new community. Within months my financial world is supported and thriving, new business opportunities appeared rapidly and fuelled the transition to now. I feel more understood by humans I choose to have in my world. My spiritual team is in place and I actively engage in activities that ensure I stay in alignment. The doors opened to support my energy and health with exactly the right natural treatments to heal my body. Investment opportunities appeared rapidly and I am able to move forward rapidly with new ventures. It is like the floodgates opened when I took the time to be brave and go there to the depths of truth. I have learnt leverage and now am living a beautiful version of life. Why would I not want to embrace being human now!"*

*MIA MUNRO*

Leverage is the master of expansion and yet when we see life in a linear fashion it is often forgotten. I have witnessed many go through enormous life changes, sometimes devastating, dealing with major illnesses to the loss of those they love. Loss of companies, business partnerships go pear shaped and major market disruption ultimately steer their steady vehicle into the red zone.

The one element that supported those leaders who made it through was their ability to leverage in life. They don't live in a box with a crazy structure with no room to breathe, they create structures and models that allow for things to get stretched! They are bold and courageous and expect change. Leveraging is important to all elements of life, not just financial.

*"I have experienced this in my life in a big way with often the ability to take anything from a month to a few years off full time dedication to my work and yet I have still been able to lead and still maintain my network for future expansion. Now that's freedom!"*

*MIA MUNRO*

Leveraging without a doubt begins with your belief systems. So we do need to unpack these to be able to expand through.

Growing up I guess I was taught leverage through my family over time. My initial years of life living in Nuku'alofa in Tonga: Mum and Dad had relocated us there so Dad could take up a position as headmaster at the school there. Mum, Dad, and us four children all headed off on an adventure and in this time Mum still managed to do major community work. Mum had my sister who lived with an intellectual disability, my two ratbag brothers, and angelic me. (Ha! My book, my version!) We had an important member of our family, Liliane, who was our nanny. To this day I feel joy when I think of her. At 40 I flew back to Tonga and was reunited with the woman who loved me and brought me up alongside Mum. What a joy to have her hug me and remember her love at that age. Mum got leverage. To manage four children in a foreign country she had to become an expert at this.

Later in life, I always looked to how I could leverage my experience. So work trips became working holidays. I often chose to live in locations that at the end of the day were holiday locations people travelled to. I used to joke about my refusal to clean my house; perhaps that is why I did not fit the traditional marriage role! (Hehe!) If I could get a cleaner in for $30/hour depending on when and where and I could make $100+ /hour why would I ever clean? You may say well, not everyone can make that money and perhaps that is true, but I couldn't initially either, it became a need to make it.

I always saw multiple applications to many things... it was just in my nature but often when I entered relationships they would have a'struggle mindset' imprinted, work hard, die early, or even slavery mindsets. Tough to thrive within those when my make-up was so extremely different.

In business, I always saw multiple pathways and have always had multiple income streams. And often not even large sums of income but more than enough to cover essential downtime and team support. This gave me years to heal myself, look after my sister, and be on adventures.

Trust is required if you are going to leverage. Micro managing and control will never give you freedom. Living in fear of everything will make life hard work!

There is always support you can access if you need it but some prefer martyrdom than creating solutions! We all have the capacity to change the way we create and grow, it's a choice we can make.

A multiple income approach is a mindset. And not necessarily easy for everyone to do. It is a choice. Divorces do happen and women or men are left with no careers and no income streams. Illness is real for most; with viral strains taking down even the most committed to health.

Exhaustion or what we call spiritual upgrades are happening at a fast rate and often come in the form of major physical symptoms or emotional crashes.

So it is not a bad pathway to consider as you plan out your needs. If what you need is more options then I encourage you to consider online businesses or alternative income streams.

They have been my saviour for years. I am happy to share the models I have done. Some have worked well, others not. I can give you a balanced view when we connect online.

If our money world is stabilised to at least have the basics covered we relax a little more. We then are in a position to consider new flows of income and even contribution projects. So I encourage you to go on an adventure of discovery and be open to new ways of doing business> Industries you may have tried prior now thrive in new ways so be open.

I have built a number of online businesses such as affiliate marketing models which have always served me well, online training programmes, product-based businesses, blogging, network marketing companies, and online retail. And I have partnered and learned from the very best with each strategy. Consider what you maybe curious about and in our online community I can share links to different options.

I see pros and cons to them all. Some have so many barriers to entry that they put many people off, some are too technically demanding, and some require lots of wisdom in specific areas.And some are people focused and some more online behind the scenes. Selection should factor in your energetic and self needs first!

In our community I can share many with you, for you to choose. I will only share ethical companies acting out of integrity. I have a strong discernment and know this industry well.

To take on the mindset of leveraging is essential because as we mentioned earlier pain and pleasure are your friends. Partnerships and people can be your greatest assets!

## Leverage—Simple Activities to Get You Started

1. Write a list of what you need to leverage most! Be clear about this. Is it TIME, MONEY, RESOURCES, SKILLS, SUPPORT, etc.
2. Write a 1, 2, 3 plan on your enquiries to gain information or understanding (collect information before saying it is not possible)
3. Schedule timelines to fulfil this journey of enquiry
4. Make a decision based on being informed
5. Seek the right support to progress!

# CHAPTER 10

# A WHOLE NEW YOU

*"Here is your opportunity to emerge as a new you. An upgraded version. A more connected version. Your soul can be alive and free. Your life reflects abundance and truth. Your relationships begin to flourish in new ways"*

Writing a book is an incredible journey in itself. It is my second book but my experience was completely different. It both energised me and caused me to have to meditate more than ever to drop into creation zone. And also to manage the amount of energy that was produced through creativity. It downloaded very fast and I found a big part of me go through a profound healing avenue with it. I understand why some people choose to journal their thoughts onto paper to have them out and clear to see.

I highly recommend the process of writing to unpack as it requires one to be so present and still, creative, honest, and exploratory. For this one it allowed me to download from a pure space. It evolved as I wrote, as I did too. The advancements in my life since I wrote the first chapter of this book are mind blowing. So here is my update. Some added thoughts, ideas, and evidence about this incredible formula which continues to amaze me. Simple yet so complex.

A summary of my journey with the whole self philosophy fully activated! Then it's your time to complete your summary!

Wealth: I have been able to recognise the power of my genius and the energy flow that is associated with expressing this. Making money alone just for the purpose of making money nearly always depletes my energy. I choose only models that support my feminine expression of truth. This book is one of my vehicles to raise awareness of the need as humans to make deliberate choices to create enriched lives. This also actively raises funds for my Social Enterprise MIAKO which will fund more education in the field of social entrepreneurship and community development both locally and internationally in the near future.

I have an Amazon business online which is leveraged in a partnership and outsourced, I have a Network Marketing business which has a powerful health treatment which has accelerated my recovery. I am in negotiations for partnerships with world class promoters of education for the future. My consulting business and upcoming retreats are mapped and ready for 2020 expansion. Strong Joint Venture partnerships in place and multiple investments online with new types of apps and disruptive models to support my re-entry into property investing.

ALL my wealth choices allow me to live in a highly nourishing environment daily.

This has all been created within a conscious reinvention period of four to six months.

**Self:** I have found a new woman beneath the old armour, the past memories, the pain and suffering, all it means to be human. I have accessed a deeper consciousness, awareness of my part within the whole and all the parts that make me whole. I have found a peace at being human and I have chosen to be here fully and experience this life as a spirit experiencing a human experience fully. I can access wisdom with ease, my empathy is high, and my boundaries even higher. My heart is wide open and free to feel deeply. I express myself openly and beam smiles, laughter and joy. I have found music again and begun my training to develop my vocal healing abilities. This is liberating.

**Energy**: I have healed my thyroid and autoimmune disease and recognise these are triggers my body has given me to take note of. My body signals very quickly a need to heal or upgrade and I listen. I access energy in multiple ways now daily. I listen and respond to my energetic needs rather than forced time frames in the three dimensional world we live in. I am diligent with my special health practices and take powerful redox signalling molecules and CBD oil daily. The response to my energy is beyond my belief. I am grateful daily for my energy and will never take it for granted again.

**Community:** This is building every day full of stunning new friends and amazing business partners. I welcome in new people. The Human Reinvention Formula Community is growing at a rapid rate and brings openness, love, and joy. I welcome you in.

**Contribution:** MIAKO the social enterprise is being reinvented and growing beautifully and beginning to support more social impact projects have the education they need to thrive for the long term. 100% profits from this book will assist in funding new students into education and expand our reach. Our new products are designed and ready to be manufactured. I feel actively in alignment and cannot wait to share with you all the sustainable products in production.

Today I hand in my manuscript to my publisher. It is 11th October 2019, it is the four-year anniversary of the passing of my beautiful sister Marnie. This symbolises a very sacred moment in time for me. The day I found my voice and true expression. The day I celebrate finding real joy and the gift of love.

May courage rear its head and allow you to go on a mission that serves your highest good. Be bold yet vulnerable. Face the truth and find your expression in this lifetime so your next version may be extraordinary. True evolution—what we are for.

It will not look like anyone else's and likely few will understand the needs of your new self as you do.

I hope this book opens your heart and allows you to be able to feel deeply into your truth. Love your version of life. Create wealth beyond your current financial ceiling and a connection with yourself. I hope your energy finds new heights and you are supported in all ways. Maybe even find space to contribute out in the world.

This is your birthright!

See you inside the online community x

# CHAPTER 11

# RESOURCES FOR YOU TO ACCESS

1. **Activation Checklist**

2. **Activation Map**

3. **Human Reinvention Design Plan**

4. **Active Meditations for Busy Minds**

5. **Disruption Tools**

And online you will find many more surprises!

You have now begun to work through the three stages comprised of three parts. We hope you have also now accessed the online community so we can continue to support you!

In our supported programmes this process can be dramatically accelerated through support and connection.

Remember, reinvention is a process.

Imagine if you were to fully activate your life, what would it truly be like?

See you soon!

Other resources are available through the Human Reinvention Formula community.

We will run retreats and events in the future; go to the online community for all information. Join us at www.miamunro.com

# CHECKLIST

Review each stage below to allow you to check in and follow through.

| | | |
|---|---|---|
| | **1. Unpack your current reality**<br><br>Have you unpacked themes, restrictions and blocks happening for you? Can you define the core area you need to reinvent first? Find the PRIORITY area. | YES  NO |
| **ACTIVATE** | **2. Disrupt to thrive long term**<br><br>Have you disrupted old paradigms and created new ones to operate within? Have you decided on a more sustainable model for your future? | YES   NO |
| | **3. Upgrade to reinvent**<br><br>Have you created your creed, manifesto and/or one-pager to complete new human reinvention design plan? | YES   NO |

| | | |
|---|---|---|
| | **4. Reveal your current resources**<br><br>Have you revealed your personal value from your past experience? What resources are available to you? What is their value? Can you see a richness in these? | **YES   NO** |
| **COLLABORATE** | **5. Define your people**<br><br>Are you clear who your people are and their value in your life?  Can you see what is not serving you? Do you need to create space to build new connections that align to your new pathway? | **YES   NO** |
| | **6. Build and trade value**<br><br>Have you defined your personal value, what you need and how you will trade value? Do you need to delve into more exploration around this? Go beyond the obvious. | **YES   NO** |

| | | |
|---|---|---|
| **EXPAND** | **7. Open up to possibilities**<br><br>Have you captured your true needs over the next seven days, 14 days, three, six, & 12 months? Have you opened to alternative opportunities and pathways? | YES  NO |
| | **8. Structure for expansion**<br><br>Have you created a three, six, 12 month focus plan? Do you have structures in place to track and measure each area for expansion? Have you scheduled evidence-based time to allow yourself to see progress? | YES  NO |
| | **9. Leveraging strategies**<br><br>Have you defined potential partnerships, systems for growth, and investment vehicles to fund you ongoing? Have you opened to new ways to move forward? Have you made contact to enquire about what is possible? | YES NO |
| | **10. Reinvention**<br><br>Transition into your new upgraded level with a deep understanding of being human. Perfectly imperfect! Do you have sustainable strategies that support your needs? Are you now reaching out to connect with new community connections and expanding relationships? Are your wealth vehicles in place to begin expansion? | YES NO |

# CHAPTER 12

# MESSAGES OF THANKS

*"The most courageous humans do the work most shy away from. They face the call to expand and embrace the pleasure. They are mighty in their beliefs and proud of their ability to reinvent themselves time and time again. They hold a glimpse of possibility when in the trenches and a determination to live beyond fear. These leaders will impact humanity through impacting their own lives first. These are the leaders who will transform our world"*

*MIA MUNRO*

## FROM LEADERS, PEERS, AND CLIENTS!

I share these messages from leaders, peers, and clients who I have engaged in throughout my career. The Human Reinvention Formula is the combination of over 15 years of work and research in many countries. And with each human life and business I have been able to support upgrades. These messages date back as early as 2010 and all hold relevance to this journey.

Thank you to all those who responded to my call to receive your thoughts! They mean so much to me. You are all a significant part of this journey. For many of you, I look forward to the next 15 years transforming this world we live in, the communities and individuals!

"I met Mia Munro through an event she was featured at many years ago. We soon became colleagues and friends. We have co-presented at many events and international retreats over the years. Mia's energy is unstoppable. I have witnessed her personal and professional reinvention over the years and am in awe of her determination to continually uplevel with each and every human experience. She is a strong leader and I firmly believe we will see more of her internationally in the coming months and years with the launch of her exciting new book.

I cannot recommend her highly enough. She is a deeply compassionate and heart-centred leader."

**Elphie Coyle**
**Creator, Polymath and Chairman**

"We met online while I was in the US. You were a key mentor for me as I set up my company. Throughout this process you offered that rare combination of power, patience, warmth, compassion, and enthusiasm. The few times we've met face to face you've been a true joy, both grounded and dynamic, and an inspiration for me to witness the heart-centred values an entrepreneur can embody."

**Alexander Thumm**
**Founder of Lamplight Forest**

"Mia changed the entire trajectory and quality of my life and entrepreneurial vision with three simple words back in 2010: Connection, Contribution, and Collaboration. Mia's guiding principles and transformational work empowered me to lead myself from broken, burnt out, and disconnected to today where I am glowing, free, and full of love. I am surrounded by aligned, purpose-driven business partners who all have people, the planet, and profit as their driving motivations."

**Kelly Quinn**
**Director – Kelly Quinn Consulting**

"Mia's life path has always taken her to more extremes than the average. High highs, low lows. It has stretched and pushed you in every way and through it all, you continue to grow, evolve, heal, step back into life and into another level that I rarely see people do. I have seen you reinvent yourself countless times, often through necessity; that said, many who experience similar events don't do that and stay stuck even though they really need to reinvent themselves. Mia never stays stuck, it's not in her to stay in anything for too long, which has been a saving grace. She experiences, she learns, she teaches and she leads, she embodies.

That's what she does and her extreme life has helped her to help even more people; those who only ever experience a mild version of her life, to those who experience the similar extreme, it makes Mia highly relatable."

**Rachel Wilson**
**Source 4 Shift**

# My Reinvention Team

*To all the other angels dressed in human clothing, thank you.*
*To all of my incredible healing team, you are incredible beings and our journey goes on. Thank you.*
*To my business colleagues and mentors who supported me at all stages, thank you.*

I have never overcome any major life shift without an incredible team of brilliant people who have supported my reinvention, even some who may not be aware of just how powerful they are! Some of these angels are people I have paid for support and many are people who have seen my light and decided to help me get back on my feet and fly even higher than ever before.

To these people, thank you from the depths of my heart! I am here and thriving today because of you! I appreciate you.

# Self + Community

Rach and Kerry—Your emotional guide and amazingly patient ears have listened for hours to my pain, my stories, and my heart yearning. You have held me strong when I have fallen and you have never faulted your belief in me. For this I will always be grateful.

Simon—You remind me of my warrior spirit and to never give up.

Emily—Deep-hearted support and mirror for love has allowed me to feel real love again.

Cheryl—Your divine support will never be forgotten, a real live angel who I respect deeply.

Roechelle—For bringing laughter into my life and your straight-up approach to life keeps me grounded.

Alissa—Post DV you treated my PTSD immediately with acutonics, the most incredible tools. Your care, compassion, and love has elevated me to new heights. You helped me listen to my soul.

Naomi—Your regular loving check-ins during my toughest days were so valued even when you had your own path to transcend.

Mikaela — Your belief in me and reminding me of my strength has been highly valued.

Sepp and Jesca—Your kind hearts and deep resonance with my journey gave me hope.

Sarah Louise ----We met briefly, you guided me at pivotal moments and I found a deeply connected woman who could meet me right where I was. Deeply grateful.

To new friends who have entered my life only during this next chapter and whom see me for who I am today, here's to many adventures.

And my family who have watched me hit rock bottom and continue to get back up and fly higher than ever before. I love you and am grateful. X

## Energy Team

I feel I need to mention a few powerful health modalities and products that accelerated my healing!

Here are some that supported my journey:

Regenerative Clinic, Medical Intuitive, Chiropractor/Kinesiologist, Acupuncture, Acutonics, Massage, Lightbody Activations, Energetic Healings, Sound Healing, Breathwork, Spinal Decompression Therapy, Yin Yoga, Magnesium Pools, Ocean Swimming, Infrared saunas,

CBD Oil, Redox Signalling Molecules, IV Vitamin C Infusions and many Natural Supplements.

Just in case they may be of help to you too. Make contact with my team if you need more information. We can direct you to the right people or modalities for what you need right now…

# Wealth

Contact us for more information on the online businesses we have experienced.

I am fortunate to be amongst some incredibly talented and wealthy entrepreneurs and investors and have created multiple joint venture and affiliate partnerships. If you seek a new wealth vehicle I can direct you to people I trust fully and also give you access to special pricing.

I have worked business in the fields of online products, travel, energy-producing products, New age property businesses, share trading and social entrepreneurship education.

In an industry that has created some confusion and a lack of trust, allow us to support you see what is real and worth investing in.

# About Mia Munro

Mia Munro is passionate about activating human beings to fuel their lives, business and projects for a more sustainable experience of life.

Through her 15 years as a transformational mentor, international speaker, author, online educator and social entrepreneur she has assisted thousands of human beings to activate new pathways that fuel their life, business, and projects.

Having built a seven-figure profiling system, spoken on stages worldwide, and authored her first book *Get Real,* she sees no limits in what is possible.

Her Human Reinvention Formula is the work of 15 years of real world experience in her own life. She supports the activation of old paradigms and gives you a seamless pathway to walk to upgrade your human experience.

She is a New Zealander who calls Australia home. She lives in Noosa, Queensland and is passionate about her fur babies, wildlife that frequent this area, and being deeply connected to spirit. Her love for music fuels much of her joy in life and she is deeply connected to humanity.

To find out more go to www.miamunro.com or join the supportive online community at: https://www.facebook.com/groups/humanreinventionformula/

# 100% PROFITS
## GO TO MIAKO

100% profits from this book will go to the MIAKO project, a Social Enterprise founded by Mia Munro in 2015. MIAKO was created to support the reinvention and development of leaders who wish to make a measurable difference through innovative and world-changing projects.

Mia has been actively involved in the creation of many Social Enterprises and with a background in not-for-profits, she is determined to shift the mindset of leaders who want to grow these projects. We do not need more of the same charities fighting for the same grants and donors, we need to innovate and create sustainable projects that can fund themselves, removing the dependence on donations and limited grants.

An online education platform was developed that activates leaders to disrupt and expand socially conscious projects into sustainable models to serve humanity.

MIAKO is developing a range of ethical and sustainable products which are sold online. These products will fund the creation of more education ongoing and support services for leaders.

MIAKO was put on hold during Mia's recent reinvention so she could return and immerse herself in the MIAKO project supported by the upgraded foundations, structures, and team for the future.

Please share this book so we may fund MIAKO and then give back to our valued communities locally, nationally, and internationally.

We thank you in advance for your contribution.

# THERE ARE MANY WAYS TO BEGIN YOUR REINVENTION JOURNEY!

1. JOIN our FREE online community at https://www.facebook.com/groups/humanreinventionformula/

2. ACCESS FREE Resources at www.miamunro.com

3. REQUEST a FREE personalised consultation with one of our team at hrf@miamunro.com

4. ENQUIRE about our ONLINE Human Reinvention Formula Assisted Program at hrf@miamunro.com

5. REGISTER for more information about ACTIVATION EVENTS and RETREATS at www.miamunro.com

# NOTES

# NOTES

# NOTES

# NOTES

# NOTES

# NOTES

# NOTES